Diseases and Disorders

Dyslexia

by Arda Darakjian Clark

LUCENT BOOKS
An imprint of Thomson Gale, a part of The Thomson Corporation

THOMSON
GALE

Detroit • New York • San Francisco • San Diego • New Haven, Conn.
Waterville, Maine • London • Munich

THOMSON
———✦——— ™
GALE

LIBRARY OF CONGRESS CATALOGING-IN-PUBLICATION DATA

Clark, Arda Darakjian, 1956–
    Dyslexia / by Arda Darakjian Clark.
        p. cm. — (Diseases and disorders)
    Includes bibliographical references and index.
    Contents: The nature of dyslexia—Theories of dyslexia—Identifying dyslexia—Treating dyslexia—Living and coping with dyslexia.
    ISBN 1-59018-040-2 (hardcover : alk. paper)
    1. Dyslexia—Juvenile literature. I. Title. II. Series: Diseases and disorders series.
LB1050.5.C547 2005
371.91′44—dc22

                                                                            2004014704

Printed in the United States of America

Table of Contents

Foreword   4

Introduction
    A Reading and Learning Disability   6

Chapter 1
    The Nature of Dyslexia   10

Chapter 2
    Theories of Dyslexia   23

Chapter 3
    Identifying Dyslexia   41

Chapter 4
    Treating Dyslexia   57

Chapter 5
    Living and Coping with Dyslexia   73

    Notes   89
    Glossary   94
    Organizations to Contact   96
    For Further Reading   99
    Works Consulted   101
    Index   107
    Picture Credits   111
    About the Author   112

"The Most Difficult Puzzles Ever Devised"

C HARLES BEST, ONE of the pioneers in the search for a cure for diabetes, once explained what it is about medical research that intrigued him so. "It's not just the gratification of knowing one is helping people," he confided, "although that probably is a more heroic and selfless motivation. Those feelings may enter in, but truly, what I find best is the feeling of going toe to toe with nature, of trying to solve the most difficult puzzles ever devised. The answers are there somewhere, those keys that will solve the puzzle and make the patient well. But how will those keys be found?"

Since the dawn of civilization, nothing has so puzzled people—and often frightened them, as well—as the onset of illness in a body or mind that had seemed healthy before. A seizure, the inability of a heart to pump, the sudden deterioration of muscle tone in a small child—being unable to reverse such conditions or even to understand why they occur was unspeakably frustrating to healers. Even before there were names for such conditions, even before they were understood at all, each was a reminder of how complex the human body was, and how vulnerable.

While our grappling with understanding diseases has been frustrating at times, it has also provided some of humankind's most heroic accomplishments. Alexander Fleming's accidental discovery in 1928 of a mold that could be turned into penicillin has resulted in the saving of untold millions of lives. The isolation of the enzyme insulin has reversed what was once a death sentence for anyone with diabetes. There have been great strides in combating conditions for which there is not yet a cure, too. Medicines can help AIDS patients live longer, diagnostic tools such as mammography and ultrasounds can help doctors find tumors while they are treatable, and laser surgery techniques have made the most intricate, minute operations routine.

This "toe-to-toe" competition with diseases and disorders is even more remarkable when seen in a historical continuum. An astonishing amount of progress has been made in a very short time. Just two hundred years ago, the existence of germs as a cause of some diseases was unknown. In fact, it was less than 150 years ago that a British surgeon named Joseph Lister had difficulty persuading his fellow doctors that washing their hands before delivering a baby might increase the chances of a healthy delivery (especially if they had just attended to a diseased patient)!

Each book in Lucent's Diseases and Disorders series explores a disease or disorder and the knowledge that has been accumulated (or discarded) by doctors through the years. Each book also examines the tools used for pinpointing a diagnosis, as well as the various means that are used to treat or cure a disease. Finally, new ideas are presented—techniques or medicines that may be on the horizon.

Frustration and disappointment are still part of medicine, for not every disease or condition can be cured or prevented. But the limitations of knowledge are being pushed outward constantly; the "most difficult puzzles ever devised" are finding challengers every day.

A Reading and Learning Disability

Dana remembers how excited her five-year-old son, Brian, was about starting kindergarten. Brian already knew the alphabet by heart and loved singing the alphabet song. He also loved looking through picture books and listened intently as his parents read to him. Dana and her husband, Tom, were excited too. They were certain that their bright and imaginative son would do well in school.

By the time Brian was in second grade, however, it became clear that he was having trouble learning to read. Brian struggled when sounding out words, made many mistakes as he read, and could not grasp basic spelling rules. He was frustrated by his inability to read well and became embarrassed when he realized that some of his classmates made fun of him. Brian remembers feeling "like I was really stupid and it bothered me that the kids in class thought I was dumb, too."[1] Brian's excitement about school turned into anxiety, and he began asking his parents if he could stay home instead.

Brian's parents wondered why a bright boy like Brian would struggle in school. They decided to visit his classroom. Dana recalls that on the day they visited, "the teacher had group reading where each child would read a passage to the whole group. When it came to Brian's turn, he began stumbling over his words and the other kids started to comment and giggle—it was horrifying. I realized we had to do something to help Brian."[2]

Brian's teacher suggested that he be evaluated by the school psychologist to find out the cause of his difficulty. Brian's parents agreed, and Brian took a series of tests. As his parents expected, the tests revealed that Brian was a bright boy, with above-average intelligence. The tests also revealed that Brian had a learning disorder called dyslexia.

What Is Dyslexia?

Dyslexia is the term used to describe the extreme difficulty some people experience with reading. People who have dyslexia are referred to as dyslexics. Researchers believe that dyslexia is a neurological, or brain-based, disorder. Dyslexics are neither mentally retarded nor slow learners, however. They have a specific problem with reading. Dyslexia expert Sally E. Shaywitz states that dyslexic children are "well-intentioned boys and girls—including very bright ones," who "experience significant difficulty in learning to read, through no fault of their own."[3]

Difficulties in reading do not only affect a person's ability to read. Since reading is a basic skill necessary for learning all subjects, students who have trouble reading are likely to have trouble in all school subjects. As dyslexic students move up in grades, they find it difficult to keep up in subjects such as social studies

Dyslexia can dramatically interfere with a child's intellectual development. Without special attention, dyslexic children struggle in the classroom and fall behind their peers.

and science because of their limited reading skills. For many dyslexics, what begins as a specific reading disability evolves into a general learning disability.

Dyslexic students do not outgrow their reading disability on their own. They must receive timely and appropriate help so they can learn to read. Even after they learn to read, dyslexia continues to be a lifelong challenge for dyslexics, who must develop strategies for living with their condition.

Overcoming Dyslexia

When a student is diagnosed with dyslexia, a special educational plan, called an individualized education program (IEP), is prepared. In Brian's case, his parents, his teacher, and the school psychologist jointly prepared an IEP for Brian so he would receive special and focused instruction to improve his reading. In addition, his parents enrolled him in a computer-aided program specifically designed to help children with dyslexia.

In June 2004 Brian completed fifth grade. His mother, Dana, says he is struggling less with his reading and writing and looking forward to middle school. Dana also says that although Brian does not read as fluently as his classmates, he is no longer fearful and frustrated by reading.

Brian's attitude toward school has also improved. His mother describes how he received help from an unexpected source: "In fourth grade, Brian discovered music. He can read any music, play anything, and play like he has played for years. He now plays sax, clarinet, and piano."[4] Brian's father, Tom, adds that while Brian's dyslexia may keep him from getting A's in his academic classes, he and his parents have found hope and joy in his musical talents.

It is not unusual for dyslexics to display talents such as Brian's gift for music. Many dyslexics are gifted in drawing, painting, sculpture, graphic arts, music, drama, architecture, and athletics. Famous dyslexics include actors Tom Cruise and Whoopi Goldberg, Olympic gold medalist Greg Louganis, and cartoonist and Disney founder Walt Disney. Discovering strengths and talents can help dyslexics feel better about themselves and recognize

Dyslexics can overcome their learning disabilities and lead successful lives. Actor Tom Cruise is one of several famous entertainers to suffer from dyslexia.

that their struggles with reading do not have to interfere with their success in life.

Difficulty learning to read is a serious problem. Being tested for dyslexia may be alarming and embarrassing at first. However, once dyslexics and their families understand what dyslexia is and that it can be overcome, they feel some relief. It helps dyslexics to know that they are not lazy or stupid, but that they have a specific difficulty with reading. It helps them to know that, despite their disability, they can aspire to higher education and rewarding careers as adults. Understanding the nature of dyslexia is a necessary first step in order to treat the disorder and find strategies for living with it. As Shaywitz states, "The greatest stumbling block preventing a dyslexic child from realizing his potential and following his dreams is the widespread ignorance about the true nature of dyslexia."[5]

Chapter 1

The Nature of Dyslexia

Most students learn to read before they reach fourth grade. In time, as they continue to read, they become fluent readers. They are able to focus on the meaning of the words they read as opposed to figuring out how to read them. Some students, however, find learning to read a tremendous challenge. For them, reading, understanding what they read, and spelling are very difficult. This extreme difficulty with words is called dyslexia. The word *dyslexia* comes from the Greek words *dys*, meaning "difficult," and *lexis*, meaning "words." Dyslexia is sometimes referred to as developmental dyslexia since it is a disorder that interferes with the development of children. Dyslexia is also commonly referred to as a reading disability.

It is not unusual for students to make mistakes in reading, spelling, or speaking. Even skilled readers make occasional mistakes. What separates dyslexics from readers who make occasional mistakes is the extreme degree of difficulty that dyslexics have with words. In addition, while nondyslexic children improve their reading skills year after year, dyslexic children struggle and fall behind their classmates. Unless dyslexic children receive special help for their reading disability, they continue to have difficulty reading throughout school and into adulthood.

Primary Traits in Dyslexia

Dyslexics exhibit a large range of symptoms related to their difficulty with words. They read slowly and make many mistakes as they read. Sometimes they make mistakes by switching letters in words. For example, a dyslexic might read the word *from* as *form* or the word *now* as *won*. Sometimes dyslexics mispronounce words by substituting one vowel for another. An example would be reading the word *pen* as *pin*. When reading aloud, dyslexics hesitate and stumble over words, and despite their sincere and intense efforts to read, they make many mistakes.

Dyslexics may also have difficulty understanding what they read. This difficulty may occur even when dyslexics fully know the meaning of the words they are reading. According to reading expert G. Reid Lyon, poor comprehension occurs because dyslexics "take far too long to read the words, leaving little energy for remembering and understanding what they have read."[6]

Along with difficulty in reading, dyslexics have trouble with spelling. While spelling errors are common for beginning readers, dyslexics often have very unusual spelling. For example, while a nondyslexic child might incorrectly spell the word *pamphlet* as *pamflet*, a dyslexic child might spell it as *pflem*.

People with dyslexia do not have trouble speaking or understanding what is said to them. At times, however, dyslexics have difficulty remembering specific words. A dyslexic child who

A young student spells words on the blackboard. As a result of their disability, dyslexics typically have great difficulty with spelling.

cannot remember the word *hat*, for example, might say something like "you know, the thing, um, the thing you wear on your head." Sometimes dyslexics substitute similar-sounding words for the ones they need. A dyslexic child might say *library* instead of *liberty* or *mellow* instead of *meadow.* Mitch, for example, is a fourteen-year-old who has dyslexia. His thirteen-year-old sister, Lynn, describes Mitch's difficulties mixing up words and letters:

> Mitch's hardest subject is reading. . . . He doesn't like to read that much. . . . Actually, he thinks reading is a waste of time. He also has trouble with letters. He confuses them. Even when he talks, he'll say words backwards or say things mixed up. Like, he'll say "red crushed peppers" instead of "crushed red peppers." And, one time, I had a social studies project about Bakersfield, California. Mitch knew all the answers, but he kept calling the place Boxerfield.[7]

Secondary Traits in Dyslexia

Although difficulty in reading and spelling are the primary indications of dyslexia, research has shown that at least some dyslexics share other traits. Some dyslexics have unusual difficulty with motor skills, a condition known as dyspraxia. Common difficulties include lack of coordination in hopping, skipping, catching and throwing balls, and riding bicycles. Fine motor skills required for activities such as tying shoelaces, buttoning shirts, and holding pencils and pens may also be imprecise. For some dyslexics, handwriting is very awkward. Some researchers believe that dyslexics write illegibly because they are uncertain of the spelling of words, but others contend that dyslexics have poor control over their fingers as they write.

Some dyslexics have difficulty orienting themselves to the world around them. They may, for example, turn left when they are asked to turn right. They may have trouble understanding directional concepts such as north, south, east, and west. Some have difficulty learning to tell the time from an analog clock because they struggle with the concept of clockwise movement. Others find organizing

Dyslexics may be challenged to master fine motor skills such as tying shoelaces, holding a pencil, or buttoning clothes.

their belongings and managing time to be troublesome.

Sequencing can also be difficult for some dyslexics. They may, for instance, have difficulty understanding multistep directions in recipes or toy-assembly instructions. Some researchers believe that impaired sequencing may be responsible for the mistakes they make in reading. For example, a child who reads the word *sung* as *snug* may have problems with sequencing the letters in words.

Some students with dyslexia also have trouble with math. Students who have difficulty sequencing, for example, may have trouble remembering formulas and equations needed for completing calculations. Some dyslexics mix up signs for addition, subtraction, multiplication, and division. Solving word problems is especially difficult for dyslexics because their reading disability interferes with understanding the problems.

Learning to read is especially difficult for dyslexics who also have attention-deficit/hyperactivity disorder (ADHD). ADHD is a behavioral disorder characterized by restlessness and impulsiveness. Learning to read requires focus and concentration, and for dyslexics who already have difficulty reading, not being able to focus and concentrate makes their problem even worse. Researchers estimate that two out of every five dyslexics have ADHD.

Although some dyslexics have many of these secondary traits, the key indicator of dyslexia remains difficulty with words. Someone who is disorganized, has trouble with math, or has ADHD but who does not have trouble reading or spelling would not be considered dyslexic. However, someone who has no difficulty other than reading or spelling is likely to be dyslexic.

An Unexpected Problem

Students with dyslexia are regularly frustrated by their reading disability. They know that they are trying hard, but their teachers, parents, and classmates do not always realize it. Dyslexic children do not understand the nature of their own problem and blame themselves. They frequently suspect that they might be stupid. Despite this common worry, dyslexics are neither mentally retarded nor slow learners. They have average or above-average intelligence (a score at or above one hundred) as shown by standard intelligence quotient (IQ) tests.

While dyslexics have average or above-average intelligence, when it comes to reading, they score below what their intelligence level and grade level would indicate. Due to the discrepancy between intelligence and reading scores in dyslexics, researchers and educators frequently refer to dyslexia as an "unexpected" problem. In fact, according to U.S. Department of Education guidelines, children must show a discrepancy between their IQ scores and their reading scores in order to be identified as dyslexic. For example, a third-grade student who scores at or above one hundred on an IQ test but reads at kindergarten level would be suspected to be dyslexic.

Some dyslexic students score above 130 on IQ tests, a score that places them in the category of mentally gifted students. Nichole, a dyslexic student, is described by her mother:

Nichole always has marched to the beat of a different drum. She has so much sparkle and so much creativity. But, in 1st grade, I noticed some discrepancies in her intellectual capability. At the end of 2nd grade, it was standard for those in her class to be tested for gifted tendencies. The licensed school psychologist called her back to redo the visual section. She told me, "Nichole is definitely gifted with an IQ of 138, but she can't spell and can't recognize words." That was when we found out she was both gifted and dyslexic.[8]

Dyslexia is also sometimes referred to as a hidden disability because dyslexics do not have obvious physical impairments. The hidden nature of dyslexia especially applies to very bright dyslexics who have no trouble learning from oral instruction in the classroom or from educational programs on television. For example, Michael might impress everyone with his remarkable knowledge about whales, and Anna might be especially talented at playing the piano. If Michael and Anna were to have difficulty learning to read, it might not occur to their parents and teachers that these bright and talented children could be dyslexic.

Who Is at Risk for Dyslexia?

Just as dyslexia cannot be predicted by intelligence scores, it also cannot be predicted by ethnic, social, or economic background. Anyone can have dyslexia. Researchers have noticed, however, that dyslexia does seem to run in families. In studying family backgrounds of dyslexics, researchers often find other family members, such as siblings, parents, aunts, or uncles, who are also dyslexic. Several studies have shown that a range of 25 to 60 percent of parents of dyslexic children currently have, or have had, reading difficulties themselves. Conversely, only 5 percent of children whose parents are fluent readers are dyslexic. These studies have led scientists to believe that the tendency to be dyslexic is inherited, as opposed to resulting from familial habits such as avoiding reading or living in homes without books.

Dyslexia and Heredity

The clearest indication that dyslexia is probably inherited comes from a major study of twins. Since 1982 more than twenty-five hundred pairs of twins have been studied in the Colorado Learning Disabilities Research Center located in Boulder, Colorado. The twins studied include identical as well as fraternal twins. Identical twins are twins who share the same genetic makeup because they have developed from the same fertilized egg. Fraternal twins are twins who do not share the same genetic makeup because they have developed from two separate fertilized eggs. Scientists study the incidence of a trait in identical and fraternal twin pairs to determine if that trait is likely to be inherited. If a trait occurs more frequently in pairs of identical twins than in pairs of fraternal twins, the trait is likely to be inherited. Studies on reading disability have shown that the identical twin of a dyslexic is much more likely to also be dyslexic than the fraternal twin of a dyslexic. According to these research results, in two out

Most Dyslexics Are Boys

Surveys have shown that three out of four dyslexic students are boys. In some research settings, however, almost as many girls have been identified as dyslexic. Some researchers believe that while objective criteria are used to identify dyslexia in research groups, boys are more often identified as dyslexic in schools because of cultural differences in the way boys and girls are perceived by their teachers. In her book *Overcoming Dyslexia*, Sally E. Shaywitz writes that fewer girls are identified as dyslexic in schools because "well-mannered little girls who sit quietly at their seats but who, nevertheless, are failing to learn to read are often overlooked." On the other hand, Shaywitz states, boys who are "a bit rambunctious—although still within the normal range for the behavior of boys—may be perceived as having a behavior problem and referred for further evaluation."

of three pairs of identical twins, both twins had reading disabilities; in contrast, only one out of three pairs of fraternal twins had reading disabilities.

In recent years scientists have attempted to discover genes that might contribute to the occurrence of dyslexia. Genes contain hereditary information that determine specific characteristics, such as someone's eye or hair color, and they are located on threadlike strands in cells known as chromosomes. In January 2002 researchers at Oxford University in the United Kingdom, along with researchers at the Colorado Learning Disabilities Research Center, published results of a study in which they compared the genes of members of families with dyslexia against all the genetic material in human chromosomes, known collectively as the human genome. Their studies pointed to several chromosomes

---

Several recent studies, however, have confirmed that boys are indeed more likely to be dyslexic than girls. In a study published in November 2001, researchers applied four different methods for identifying dyslexia to a group of students in Rochester, Minnesota. The researchers found that, depending on the method used, boys were two to three times more likely than girls to be dyslexic. In another report, published in April 2004, four large studies of more than ten thousand children in Britain and New Zealand were described. The researchers in the four studies found that while the incidence of dyslexia among boys ranged from 18 to 22 percent, the incidence of dyslexia among girls ranged from 8 to 13 percent. According to the results of these four studies, then, boys are twice as likely to be dyslexic as girls.

Researchers do not know why dyslexia occurs more frequently in boys. It is possible that dyslexia is similar to male-pattern baldness, which is influenced by gender. Additional research is necessary before credible theories about dyslexia and gender can be advanced.

Although researchers like this one have identified the gene that may be responsible for dyslexia, they still do not understand how the faulty gene causes the disorder.

that may be the most likely locations of genes that are thought to lead to dyslexia. More recently, in August 2003, researchers in Finland announced the discovery of a single gene, identified as DYXC1, as a possible cause of dyslexia. The researchers, who had studied twenty unrelated Finnish families with a high rate of dyslexia, found that the DYXC1 gene was shortened or altered in their research subjects. Researchers are not sure how the faulty DYXC1 gene contributes to the development of dyslexia, but they believe that the gene could play a role in identifying people who might be at risk for dyslexia.

Regardless of which gene or genes are discovered to be common among dyslexic families, it is clear to researchers that heredity is a strong factor in the occurrence of dyslexia. Yet simply having a gene for dyslexia does not necessarily lead to the disorder. What a child inherits is a tendency to be dyslexic. Researchers do not know, however, why the inherited tendency leads to dyslexia for some children but not for others.

How Common Is Dyslexia?

Since 1992 the U.S. Department of Education has periodically assessed reading performance of students enrolled in both public and private schools throughout the United States. The assessments have repeatedly shown that close to 40 percent of fourth-grade students read below their grade level. Not all students who have difficulty in reading are dyslexic, though. Other rea-

Genes for Reading?

Linguists estimate that humans have been speaking for at least fifty thousand years. Compared to speech, reading and writing are relatively new skills for humans, dating back five thousand years. Archaeologists believe that written language was first developed around 3200 or 3300 B.C. by the Sumerians, a group of people who lived in what is now southern Iraq. In the following centuries, few people learned to read and write. That changed in the mid-1400s with Gutenberg's invention of the printing press, which made it possible for large numbers of books to be printed quickly. In time, more and more people learned to read and write, though it took another four hundred years before large populations of people learned to read.

One of the intriguing issues in dyslexia is that a skill as new as reading can be affected by heredity. From the standpoint of evolution, five hundred or even five thousand years is not sufficient time for humans to develop genes for reading ability or disability. When scientists speak of dyslexia being inherited, then, they do not mean that reading disability is specifically inherited. They mean that certain structures or functions of the human brain that lead to dyslexia are inherited, as determined by genes.

sons for difficulty in reading include having visual or hearing defects, brain injury, mental retardation, and behavioral disorders. Children who are raised in homes without books or who receive inadequate instruction are also at risk for reading difficulties. By contrast, a dyslexic child is a healthy, intelligent child who has had adequate opportunity to learn but who still finds it difficult to read.

Estimates for the incidence of dyslexia vary. Some researchers estimate that up to half of the children reading below grade level, or 20 percent of all children in school, may be dyslexic. Most researchers estimate that dyslexia occurs less frequently, affecting 5 to 15 percent of students. This difference in estimates occurs because of varying formulas used to identify dyslexia. In a study in Rochester, Minnesota, researchers applied four different identification formulas to the same group of reading-disabled children. They found that, depending on the formula used, the incidence rates of reading disability varied from 5.3 to 11.8 percent. Currently, 5 percent of all students enrolled in U.S. public schools, or approximately 2.3 million students, are identified as dyslexic and receive special education services for their reading disabilities. Using the most frequently cited estimate of 5 to 15 percent as the rate of incidence of dyslexia, the number of dyslexics in the U.S. population in 2004 ranges from 14.5 to 43.5 million.

The Impact of Dyslexia

Not only does dyslexia affect a large number of people, but it is also a disorder with serious consequences. Reading is a basic skill for learning. Children are taught to read in early elementary grades so they can be ready to learn by reading about a variety of subjects in upper grades. Educators refer to this process as "learning to read, reading to learn." Students who do not master reading may have difficulty in subjects such as social studies, science, and math. Dyslexia, then, is not only a reading disability but also a learning disability. In fact, it is the most common learning disability. According to the U.S. Department of Education, reading disability is the main disability for four out of every five children identified as learning disabled.

Since learning to read at a young age is essential for education and social development, dyslexics find themselves at a disadvantage in our literacy-driven society.

Reading is essential to learning, but it is also essential to success in society. G. Reid Lyon, who oversees reading research for the National Institute of Child Health and Human Development (NICHD), considers learning to read "critical to a child's overall well being." He adds, "If a youngster does not learn to read in our literacy-driven society, hope for a fulfilling, productive life diminishes. In short, difficulties learning to read are not only an educational problem; they constitute a serious public health concern."[9]

Research in Dyslexia

In view of the negative impact of dyslexia on society, the NICHD, along with other agencies such as the U.S. Department of Education, funds a vast research program dedicated to the study of reading. The purpose of the research is to understand how children learn to read, why some children have trouble reading, and how children with reading disabilities can best be helped. Researchers come from many fields, including biology, neurology, genetics, psychology, and education. These scientists work to weave together the knowledge and perspective they each have to arrive at a better understanding of dyslexia, its causes, and its treatment. The research takes place in dozens of universities, medical centers, hospitals, and research labs across the country. U.S. researchers also work closely with researchers around the world. There are large research programs in Canada, the United Kingdom, Finland, Norway, Sweden, Russia, and China.

Dyslexia has been studied for more than one hundred years. In that time, researchers and educators have advanced various theories about what dyslexia is, what causes it, and how it can be treated. Despite the extensive research, both past and current, dyslexia is a subject full of unanswered questions. Although scientists have suggested several probable causes of dyslexia, the exact cause is still in question. Educators and other researchers, meanwhile, frequently disagree on the best methods to identify and help dyslexics. Still others question whether it is necessary to separate dyslexia from reading disabilities caused by other factors such as mental retardation, lack of opportunity, behavioral issues, or lack of motivation.

Most researchers do, however, agree on a basic definition of dyslexia as an inherited reading disability in people who are of average or above-average intelligence and who have had adequate instruction. Scientists also agree that the answer to the dyslexia puzzle is in the human brain, and recent advances in medical technology have helped scientists come closer to understanding the neurological, or brain-based, nature of dyslexia.

Chapter 2

Theories of Dyslexia

Despite having studied dyslexia for more than a century, scientists have not identified the disorder's exact cause. They have, however, advanced several theories about various impairments in the brain that they believe lead to dyslexia. Most researchers believe that dyslexia results from impairments in the language processing centers of the brain. It is possible, though, that several impairments in different areas of the brain act jointly to cause dyslexia. It is also possible that a single deficit in the brain leads to dyslexia by itself or in combination with other disorders.

Dyslexia was first identified as a distinct reading disorder in the late nineteenth century. Although written language had been around then for more than five thousand years, large populations of people did not become literate until the middle of the nineteenth century. Once literacy spread among large groups, reports of people with reading difficulties emerged.

Early Research in Dyslexia

The early reading disability studies examined adults who had once been capable readers but who had lost their ability to read as a result of a tumor, a stroke, or an injury to the brain. In 1877 a German neurologist named Adolf Kussmaul was puzzled by a patient who had no trouble seeing and no apparent brain injury but who could not read words. Kussmaul referred to his patient's condition as "word blindness." The term *dyslexia* itself was first used by Rudolph Berlin, a German physician, in 1887. Berlin used the term *dyslexia* in referring to patients who had difficulty reading as opposed to patients with alexia, the complete inability to read. In 1895 James Hinshelwood, a Scottish ophthalmologist, published an essay in which he described how a highly educated teacher, who had no visual or mental defects, had woken up one day unable to read.

Hinshelwood's description of the teacher's symptoms inspired an English physician named W. Pringle Morgan to describe a case he had studied. In 1896 Morgan wrote an essay in which he described a fourteen-year-old boy named Percy:

> He has always been a bright and intelligent boy, quick at games, and in no way inferior to others of his age.
>
> His great difficulty has been—and is now—his ability to learn to read. This inability is so remarkable, and so pronounced, that I have no doubt it is due to some congenital defect. He has been at school or under tutors since he was 7 years old, and the

Children read in a New York school in this photo from the 1890s. By the late nineteenth century, large numbers of Americans had become literate.

greatest efforts have been made to teach him to read, but, in spite of this laborious and persistent training, he can only with difficulty spell out words of one syllable.[10]

Morgan was the first scientist to advance the theory that reading disability may be a congenital or inborn disorder. Morgan recognized the similarity between the symptoms he observed in Percy and the word blindness in brain-damaged adults described by Kussmaul, Berlin, and Hinshelwood. By describing Percy's difficulty as a "congenital defect," Morgan shifted the focus of reading-disability research from adults who suddenly lose their ability to read to children who have difficulty learning to read.

Awareness of Dyslexia Expands

Following the publication of Morgan's essay, other physicians, optometrists, and scientists in Europe began publishing their own studies of reading difficulty. Hinshelwood, who had initially inspired Morgan's essay, went on to study and write about many cases of congenital reading disability. His extensive work helped build awareness of dyslexia as a disorder specific to reading.

Another pioneer in dyslexia research was Samuel T. Orton, an American neurologist. Beginning in the 1920s Orton studied children with reading difficulties and made particular note of certain common symptoms. Orton noticed the symptom of reversing letters, as in reading *b* as *d* or *p* as *q*, and the symptom of mirror-image reading, as in reading *ten* as *net* or *saw* as *was*. To describe reading difficulties, Orton proposed the term *strephosymbolia*, meaning "twisted symbols," based on his theory that dyslexics reversed or twisted letters in their brains after seeing them. In time, Orton adopted the term *dyslexia*, by which reading disability came to be known.

Although most researchers no longer believe that dyslexics see letters in reverse or words in mirror image, Orton had considerable influence in making the public aware of reading difficulties. He also believed strongly that dyslexics could learn to read with appropriate instruction. Along with educator Anna Gillingham, Orton developed a teaching method for reading that is still in wide use today.

The Focus of Dyslexia Research Shifts to Language

When researchers first began to study dyslexia, they tried to understand how dyslexics failed to see. Although early researchers such as Hinshelwood and Orton realized that dyslexics did not have eye impairments, their theories still focused on visual concepts such as word blindness and twisted symbols. Beginning in the 1960s, scientists began exploring the idea that dyslexia may be related less to seeing and more to language.

Linguists, scientists who study language, believe that the capacity for language is an innate skill, born with children. Without any specific instruction in how to speak, babies begin to babble at about six months of age and begin to speak when they are about one year old. Unlike speech, reading and writing are complex skills that must be specifically taught.

Before they can read and write, children must learn the symbols for the sounds in their language. The English alphabet is an example of a symbolic code for the sounds of language. Reading

Linguists believe that babies are born with both the ability to speak and to use language. The ability to read and write, however, must be learned.

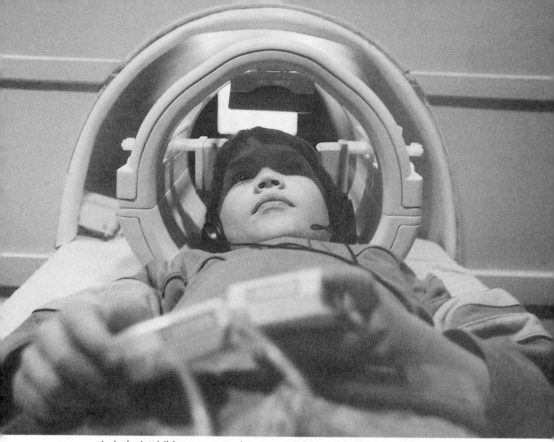

A dyslexic child prepares to have an MRI scan of his brain. MRI scans allow doctors to detect irregularities in the brains of dyslexics.

is a process of decoding or translating the written symbols of language into the sounds and meanings of words. That process of translation takes place in the brain.

Seeing the Reader's Brain

Until recent years scientists did not have appropriate scientific tools that would allow them to look inside the brain while a person read. Performing autopsies on dyslexic brains could reveal anatomical differences or obvious damage, such as lesions, in the brain. Autopsies, however, could not provide any insight about what happened in the brains of living people as they read.

Advances in medical technology have helped scientists view the human brain as certain tasks are carried out. The most recent technology used by dyslexia researchers is known as magnetic resonance imaging (MRI). MRI is a technique in which radio waves, electromagnets, and computers are used to provide detailed and clear pictures of a person's internal organs and tissues. A variation of MRI technology, known as functional MRI (fMRI), is used to measure the very rapid and subtle changes that take place in the brain as a person performs a task such as reading. When an area of the brain is hard at work, blood full of oxygen is rushed to the area. The fMRI scans show which areas of the brain are receiving fresh supplies of oxygenated blood. This fMRI technology has allowed scientists to see into the brain while both dyslexics and nondyslexics read, in order to look for differences in the brains of the two groups.

How the Brain Reads

When people read, a highly complex and coordinated process takes place in their brains. The eyes scan the words on the page and forward information, such as the color, depth, shape, and angle of the letters, to the brain. From the eyes, the two optic nerves carry the information about the letters to the thalamus, an area of the brain that acts as a type of relay station, and then to the visual cortex, an area located in the back of the brain. The brain then sees the letters.

Seeing the letters on the page is not the same as reading the letters, however. An English-speaking person who does not know Greek, for example, can see Greek letters but cannot interpret their meaning. To read, a person's brain must link the visual information it has received about the letters to the sounds and meanings of the words being read. This linkage takes place in areas of the brain known as language processing centers. The three primary language processing centers are known as the angular gyrus, Wernicke's area, and Broca's area. For most people these language processing centers are located in the left hemisphere of the brain.

Once the visual cortex has seen the letters, neural, or nerve, signals are sent forward to the angular gyrus. In this area, the visual information about the letters being read is converted into an auditory code. The auditory code then proceeds to Wernicke's area, where the brain determines the meaning of what is read.

If the reader is reading out loud, neural signals move from Wernicke's area to Broca's area. In this area, the brain prepares to vocalize, or speak, the words being read and sends signals to the motor areas of the brain that prompt the vocal cords to begin speech.

Reading, then, is a very complex process. In order to read with ease, the brain's visual cortex and language processing centers must work well together and very rapidly. Even minor impairments in the visual and language processing areas would interfere with a person's ability to read.

How the Dyslexic Brain Reads

Functional MRI scans show that dyslexics do not use the same neural-processing pathways as nondyslexics. Dyslexia expert Sally E. Shaywitz states, "Careful examination of brain activation patterns has revealed a glitch in this circuitry in dyslexic readers."[11] When nondyslexics read, the visual cortex, the angular

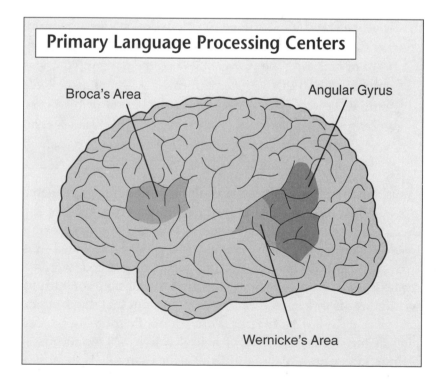

Primary Language Processing Centers

Broca's Area

Angular Gyrus

Wernicke's Area

The Discovery of Language Processing Centers in the Brain

In the mid-1800s, a major debate among scientists was whether the human brain worked as a whole or whether different parts of the brain were responsible for different functions. French physician Paul Broca and German neurologist Carl Wernicke, working separately, discovered areas of the brain that were responsible for processing language. Broca's and Wernicke's discoveries led scientists to conclude that distinct areas of the brain are specialized for specific functions.

In 1861 Broca met a patient with an unusual condition: The only word he could say was *tan*. It was clear that the patient could understand what was said to him—for example, if someone asked him for the time, he would correctly gesture with his fingers—but every verbal response he made consisted of repeating the word *tan*. When the patient (who was nicknamed Tan) died, Broca performed an autopsy on Tan's brain and discovered a lesion on the left side of his brain. Broca theorized that the area damaged in Tan's brain was an area responsible for producing speech. When Broca presented

gyrus, and Wernicke's area are all activated by oxygenated blood. When dyslexics read, most of the activity takes place in Broca's area instead of in the angular gyrus and Wernicke's area. Instead of relying on the angular gyrus and Wernicke's area—the two areas responsible for making sense of printed words—dyslexics rely on Broca's area, the area responsible for turning written words into speech. Shaywitz points out that the common trait among dyslexics of saying words under their breath is a display of the dyslexic pattern of neural activity: "One means of compensating for a reading difficulty, for example, is to subvo-

his ideas to the scientific community, not everyone was convinced. In time, however, scientists realized that Broca was right, and the area of the brain he identified came to be known as Broca's area. Tan's brain, which Broca preserved, is still kept in a museum in France.

In 1874 Wernicke identified another area of the brain involved in language. Unlike Broca's patient Tan, Wernicke's patients had no trouble speaking. In fact, they spoke without hesitation and at length. The trouble was that even though their sentences mostly followed grammatical structure, the words and phrases they strung together made no sense. Wernicke identified an area of the brain (located behind Broca's area) that he theorized was responsible for understanding the meaning of sounds and words. The area Wernicke identified came to be known as Wernicke's area.

French physician Paul Broca identified an area of the brain responsible for language.

calize (say the words under your breath) as you read, a process that utilizes a region in the front of the brain (Broca's area) responsible for articulating spoken words."[12]

Functional MRI scans have also shown that at least some dyslexics have mildly impaired processing in visual pathways known as magnocellular pathways. These pathways are located in the thalamus and are especially sensitive to motion and rapid stimuli. The role of magnocellular pathways in reading has not been clearly established, but some researchers suspect that impairment of the magnocells slows down the processing of stimuli (the words being read) and causes the thalamus to relay the information to the visual cortex in an improper sequence. Magnocellular pathways may also be responsible for eye movements, and impaired magnocells may interfere with the ability of the two eyes to work together to focus on the words being read.

Anatomical Studies

In addition to the impairments in dyslexic brains revealed by fMRI scans, studies of autopsied brains have shown certain anatomical differences between nondyslexic and dyslexic brains. In nondyslexics, the left hemisphere of the brain, where language processing takes place, is somewhat larger than the right hemisphere. In dyslexics, the two hemispheres are the same size. Researchers theorize that dyslexics have equal-size brain hemispheres because the language processing centers in their left hemispheres are not as well developed as the left hemispheres of nondyslexics.

Studies have also shown scarring in some neurons in the language processing and auditory processing centers of dyslexic brains. Researchers suspect that these scars interfere with smooth language and auditory processing. In addition, autopsy studies have shown that magnocellular tissues in dyslexic brains appear disorganized and that the individual magnocells are smaller than in nondyslexic brains. Some researchers believe that the small size of magnocells and the disorganization in magnocellular tissues cause the magnocellular pathways to function improperly, which in turn causes improper processing of visual stimuli.

Theories of Dyslexia

In recent years, based on anatomical studies, fMRI scans, and other research, scientists have formulated several theories about dyslexia. Although scientists agree that dyslexia is a neurological disorder, the precise impairment in the brain that leads to dyslexia is still in question. The theory most widely accepted among scientists is known as the phonemic deficit theory. Other theories include the visual processing theory, the auditory processing theory, and the automaticity, or cerebellar, theory.

The Phonemic Deficit Theory

Most researchers believe that dyslexics have trouble reading because they are unable to take apart the sounds of speech in words and relate those sounds to letters in print. The inability to take apart sounds of speech is referred to as a phonemic deficit. (Some researchers refer to this as a phonological deficit.) A phoneme is the smallest distinct bit of sound. There are forty-four phonemes in spoken English. In written English, the twenty-six letters of the alphabet are used to symbolize, or stand for, the sounds of speech. Since there are more phonemes than letters, some phonemes are symbolized by consonant and vowel combinations. For example, to represent the single sound /sh/, the two letters *s* and *h* are combined. In the word *mat*, there are three phonemes, /m/ /a/ /t/, represented by the three letters *m, a, t*. The word *mash* also contains three phonemes, /m/ /a/ /sh/, but it is represented by the four letters *m, a, s, h*.

According to the phonemic deficit theory, dyslexics do not detect the three distinct sounds in a word such as *mat*. When people speak, they do not sound out each phoneme or sound separately. They make the sounds of words in quick succession and in the correct sequence. When a speaker says the word *fresh*, the phonemes /f/ /r/ /e/ /sh/ are coarticulated, or spoken together, in a particular sequence, without gaps in the sounds. For the dyslexic, it is difficult to recognize that while people do not place gaps between phonemes when they speak, phonemes are still separate sounds. Researchers believe that dyslexics also lack an awareness of the sequence of the phonemes in a word. When a dyslexic reads a word such as *enemy* as *emeny*, the mistake is made because of the dyslexic's difficulty with the sequence of phonemes in the word.

A large number of phonemic awareness tests given to dyslexics have repeatedly shown that phonemic deficits form the core of their reading difficulties. Autopsies that have shown abnormalities in the language processing centers of dyslexic brains provide additional support for the phonemic deficit theory. The strongest support for this theory comes from fMRI scans that show that dyslexics do not use the angular gyrus and Wernicke's area of the brain in the same way as nondyslexics. Shaywitz likens the new fMRI technology to that of an X-ray: "Before [fMRI scans], we could hypothesize that the child was very bright but had a real biological difficulty making him or her unable to read. Now, we can look at an imaging pattern and say, 'Aha, this is a real problem; this is as real as a broken arm that you might look at on X-ray.'"[13]

Currently, the phonemic deficit theory is the most commonly accepted theory among dyslexia researchers. There are other theories, but phonemic deficits are so prevalent in dyslexia that even supporters of other theories do not argue against their existence. As dyslexia expert Margaret J. Snowling states, "It is rare to find a dyslexic child who does not have some kind of phonological problem."[14] Researchers who promote alternative theories, however, believe that the phonemic deficit theory is not a sufficient

A teacher goes over a phonemic awareness test with a dyslexic student. Most dyslexics lack awareness of the sequence of phonemes in a word.

explanation for all of the difficulties that dyslexics face. These researchers believe that, at least for some dyslexics, visual or auditory deficits alone can cause reading disorders or worsen them. Others believe that reading disability is part of a larger syndrome that causes multiple difficulties.

The Auditory Processing Theory

Supporters of the auditory processing theory agree that the major difficulty in dyslexia is a phonemic deficit. Yet they believe that an underlying disorder in auditory or sound processing is at the root of the dyslexic's phonemic deficit. According to this theory, an auditory impairment in the brain causes the dyslexic to have difficulty processing rapidly occurring sounds, such as consonant sounds in words. This difficulty causes the dyslexic to be unable to tell the difference between the sounds of letters (as in hearing the word *big* as *pig*) and the sequences of letters in a word (as in hearing the word *elephant* as *ephelant*).

To support their theory, proponents of the auditory processing theory point to studies that have shown that dyslexic children have difficulty identifying rapidly occurring sounds. They also point to the anatomical studies that have shown scarring in auditory processing cells in dyslexic brains.

Some studies have shown that up to 50 percent of dyslexics have an auditory processing disorder. From these studies, supporters of the auditory processing theory conclude that auditory difficulties cause phonemic deficits. Supporters of the phonemic deficit theory, however, believe that although auditory processing disorders do occur alongside phonemic deficits in some dyslexics, they do not necessarily lead to phonemic deficits. Dyslexia researcher Franck Ramus states that it is "perfectly plausible that a mild auditory disorder would have an impact on the development of the phonological system." Yet he adds that the auditory disorders observed in dyslexics are "mostly unrelated to speech perception and phonological processing. . . . It also appears that auditory disorders are restricted to a subset of dyslexics . . . and that they are not necessary for a phonological deficit to arise."[15]

The Visual Processing Theory

Just as the proponents of the auditory processing theory do not dispute the phonemic deficit theory, proponents of the visual processing theory also believe that the phonemic deficit theory applies to most dyslexics. Proponents of the visual theory, however, believe that the phonemic deficit theory does not entirely explain certain difficulties encountered by dyslexics. These difficulties include transposing letters, such as in reading *won* as *now*, or transposing numerals, such as in reading *14* as *41* or *6* as *9*. Other visual difficulties reported by some dyslexics include seeing letters and words blur, merge together, or overlap as they try to read. Some dyslexics also complain that lines of text shimmer and warp and seem to disappear off the page.

According to the visual processing theory, abnormalities in the visual magnocellular pathways impair visual processing as dyslexics attempt to read. Although these impairments are mild and are usually detected in low-light levels or in unusual motion conditions, proponents believe that, as a result of these impairments, dyslexics' two eyes do not work well together. Dyslexia researchers John Stein and Vincent Walsh, two leading supporters of the visual theory of dyslexia, explain that dyslexics' "eyes are unsteady when they are attempting to view small letters; hence their vision is unstable and they tend to make visual reading errors."[16]

In support of the visual theory, researchers point to autopsy and fMRI scan results that show that dyslexics have abnormalities in their visual magnocellular pathways. Researchers have also noted that when dyslexics read with one eye closed, they make fewer visual errors. According to Stein and Walsh, reading with one eye "relieves the confusion caused by two images moving around independently."[17]

Critics of the visual theory point out that the link between abnormal visual magnocells and poor reading has not been clearly established. They also note that regardless of the role of magnocells, any theory that relates dyslexia to visual deficits would apply to a small minority of dyslexics, since for most dyslexics, the core deficit is a phonemic deficit.

Proponents of the visual processing theory maintain that the reading difficulties of dyslexics stem from defects in their visual magnocellular pathways.

The Automaticity, or Cerebellar, Theory

Automaticity is a term used to describe the potential for certain everyday tasks to become automatic. When people first learn a new skill, they focus their concentration and make a conscious effort to perform the task. As they repeat the task, they begin to give it less thought each time until the task becomes automatic. For example, someone learning a new dance consciously and deliberately repeats the steps until he or she can dance without thinking about it.

According to the automaticity theory of dyslexia, dyslexics have trouble reading because they have a deficiency in making tasks automatic. The proponents of this theory base their position on research showing that dyslexics perform poorly on tasks involving motor skills such as balance. Since the part of the brain that controls motor skills is the cerebellum, the automaticity theory is also known as the cerebellar theory.

Proponents of the automaticity theory do not disagree with the phonemic deficit theory, either. They believe, however, that the difficulty dyslexics have goes beyond the language problems described by the phonemic theory. Psychologist Angela J. Fawcett, one of the leading supporters of the automaticity theory, explains that after having observed her own dyslexic child, she "was aware that the deficits in dyslexia included, but extended far beyond, these phonological deficits." She adds: "I had noticed that there were subtle differences in the fluency with which children with dyslexia performed on all tasks." She then describes that she, along with her colleague Rod Nicolson, "formulated and tested the automatisation deficit hypothesis . . . that dyslexic children have problems in becoming automatic in any skill, whether or not it is related to reading."[18]

Some studies have shown that up to 50 percent of dyslexics show problems in coordination, balance, and other motor skills. Critics of the cerebellar theory, however, point out that children who do have motor difficulties also have other difficulties such as attention deficit disorder or dyspraxia.

Many dyslexics have problems with coordination and balance. An activity as basic as riding a bicycle can be a tremendous challenge for dyslexics.

Reconciling the Theories

Some researchers have attempted to reconcile the different theories of dyslexia. For example, Stein and Walsh have expanded on their visual processing theory and have advanced a more comprehensive theory, which they refer to as the magnocellular theory. The magnocellular theory proposes that dyslexia is caused by impaired processing of both visual stimuli, such as written words, and auditory stimuli, such as the sounds of speech. Stein and Walsh note that there are certain auditory cells that function in a manner similar to visual magnocells in the thalamus. They believe that impairments in both auditory cells and visual magnocellular pathways interfere with timely processing of auditory as well as visual stimuli. In addition, they note that auditory and visual pathways end in the cerebellum, and they believe that when those pathways are damaged, the function of the cerebellum is impaired. The impairment of the cerebellum in turn causes the motor difficulties some dyslexics have. Thus, the magnocellular theory contains elements of the visual, auditory, and cerebellar theories. Stein and Walsh acknowledge that dyslexics have phonemic deficits, but they argue that the phonemic deficit is a result of an auditory processing difficulty. Critics of the magnocellular theory, however, point out that most dyslexics display phonemic deficits without any indication of visual, auditory, or motor difficulties.

Another theory, advanced by dyslexia researchers Maryanne Wolf and Patricia Bowers, proposes that there may be three types of dyslexics. One set of dyslexics may suffer from a pure phonemic deficit, a second may have difficulty with rapid processing, and a third set may suffer from what Wolf and Bowers call a double deficit. According to the double deficit theory, some dyslexics have both a phonemic deficit and a rapid processing deficit that interferes with the quick processing of stimuli. Using tests known as rapid automatic naming (RAN), Wolf and Bowers discovered that many dyslexics score poorly in RAN tests in which they are asked to look at letters, numbers, colors, and pictures and name them as quickly as possible. Wolf and Bowers also found that dyslexics who score poorly on RAN tests and have a phonemic deficit tend to have the most difficulty in reading. More specifically, dyslexics with double deficits have trouble becoming fluent readers. According to Wolf, "A majority of children with developmental reading disabilities have significant weaknesses in naming speed from kindergarten on and . . . they go on to develop problems in reading fluency and comprehension."[19]

Some researchers believe that there is no single cause of dyslexia that applies to all dyslexics. It is possible that whereas some people have difficulty reading due to a phonemic deficit, others have visual, auditory, or cerebellar causes for their difficulty. It is also possible that several different impairments occur jointly to cause dyslexia. In other words, any or all of the various theories of dyslexia may apply to at least some dyslexics. Since dyslexics display a range of difficulties from mild to severe, it is possible that someone with mild visual impairment will have mild reading disabilities, and someone with phonemic, visual, auditory, and cerebellar deficits will have severe reading disabilities.

The Elusive Cause of Dyslexia

Despite extensive research and the advancement of various theories, scientists still do not know the exact cause of dyslexia. Although autopsies, fMRIs, and other tests have shown impairments in dyslexic brains, no one knows what causes the impairments themselves. Researchers believe that impairments occur in the brain during gestation, either due to heredity or to unknown environmental factors. Future research may reveal more specifically what causes the various impairments in the brain that have been linked to dyslexia.

While the precise cause of dyslexia eludes scientists, reading disability remains a serious problem for millions of people. Educators encounter reading disability among their students on a daily basis, and regardless of the causes of dyslexia, teachers and parents of dyslexic students need to be able to recognize the disorder and develop plans to deal with it.

Chapter 3

Identifying Dyslexia

Dyslexics display a number of characteristic symptoms that researchers believe result from their neurological impairments. All dyslexics have difficulties with language, but symptoms vary from person to person based on the precise impairment and its severity. Symptoms also vary based on the age and educational level of the person. A second-grade dyslexic student who has severe difficulty sounding out words may become the high school student who cannot keep up with reading requirements and the adult who avoids reading whenever possible.

Although the symptoms vary as a dyslexic child gets older, dyslexia itself cannot be outgrown. The condition is with the dyslexic from birth and remains with the person throughout his or her life. However, depending on when they are diagnosed and the quality of special help they receive, some of the extreme difficulty that young dyslexics face may ease as they grow up. Dyslexic children who do not get diagnosed or receive help are likely to grow into adults who continue to have difficulty reading and learning.

Symptoms in Preschoolers

Dyslexics first display symptoms as toddlers beginning to speak. According to dyslexia expert Sally E. Shaywitz, "The very first clue to dyslexia may be *a delay in speaking*."[20] Shaywitz points out that this first clue is easy to ignore since the delay may be a modest one of just a few months. While nondyslexic children typically begin speaking in phrases when they are about eighteen months old, dyslexic children may not begin speaking in phrases until they are at least two years old. Not all children who begin speaking later than their peers are dyslexic, but delayed speech may be an especially important clue for children in families with dyslexia. Shaywitz states, "A seemingly innocent speech delay may be an early warning signal of a future reading problem— especially in a family that has a history of dyslexia."[21]

In addition, preschoolers who have difficulty grasping the idea of rhymes are at greater risk for dyslexia. Such children have difficulty learning nursery rhymes and fail to understand how words such as *cat, hat*, and *mat* rhyme. Dyslexic children also add new words to their vocabulary at a slower pace than nondyslexic children. Other difficulties that may be related to dyslexia include mixing up directional words such as *up, down, in*, or *out*, and slow development of fine motor skills needed to hold pencils or small objects.

Symptoms in Kindergarten Through Fourth Grade

Dyslexic children in grades kindergarten through fourth show the symptoms most often associated with dyslexia. In the early school years, when the most important task for children is learning to read, the difficulties of dyslexic children are highlighted. Since dyslexics have difficulty relating sounds to the letters of the alphabet, they find the process of sounding words out very awkward and tiring. They also have difficulty reading basic words (such as *the, an*, and *run*) that children are expected to read by sight, without sounding out. Dyslexic children in these grades may reverse letters (such as *b* for *d*), invert letters (such as *m* for *w*), or transpose letters in words (such as *snip* for *spin*). Some children substitute similar words in meaning (such as *house* for *home*) or sound (such as *foot* for *fruit*) when they read, write, or speak. Spelling is particularly difficult for dyslexic children at this age since they do not adequately grasp the concept of specific letters being related to specific sounds.

Some dyslexic children in the early school years have difficulty with organization, telling left from right, and learning about compass points and time. Others grip pencils awkwardly

Dyslexia is often diagnosed during a child's preschool years. Children who grip pencils awkwardly and have poor handwriting may be showing signs of the disorder.

and have poor handwriting. Some are clumsy and exhibit poor coordination in playing games.

Symptoms in Fifth Through Eighth Grade

Dyslexic children in fifth through eighth grade display many of the same reading and spelling difficulties that children in early elementary grades display. As they advance through school, however, academic demands increase and dyslexic children struggle to keep up with those demands. Beginning in fifth grade, the emphasis in education shifts from learning to read to learning about geography, history, and science—all subjects that require strong reading skills. Even math may become difficult for dyslexics as they learn to solve word problems.

Since reading is such an uncomfortable task for dyslexic children, they try to avoid it whenever possible. But by doing so, they limit their exposure to new vocabulary words, correctly spelled words, and well-written sentences. For a student who already has a reading disability, the limited exposure to written language makes things worse. It becomes more and more difficult for dyslexic students to understand the increasingly complicated material they study in school.

Because advanced subjects such as geography require strong reading and comprehension skills, dyslexics often feel frustrated when studying such subjects.

Symptoms in High School and College

Keeping up with the extensive reading requirements in high school and college can be a challenge for all students. For dyslexic students, the challenge is even greater. Dyslexics need much more time to read than their classmates require, and they have difficulty understanding the material they read, partly because of the effort required just to read and partly because of inadequate vocabulary due to their avoidance of reading. Another challenge in high school and college is learning a foreign language. Dyslexic students, who are already struggling with one language, find learning foreign languages problematic.

Symptoms in Adult Dyslexics

For adult dyslexics, dealing with language continues to be difficult. Regardless of whether they have received help in school, dyslexics come to adulthood having spent many years with their learning disability. Having completed their education, adult dyslexics find it easier to avoid reading. They may, for example, pursue jobs that do not require extensive reading or writing.

Adult dyslexics who did not receive adequate help with their reading disorder often attempt to hide their difficulty. For example, they might ask a stranger in a supermarket to read a label, stating that they have forgotten their glasses at home. They might ask a dining companion to choose a meal for them instead of trying to read the menu. Some dyslexics have confessed to consistently ordering the restaurant's special of the day instead of reading the menu.

As is true for dyslexic children, the reading disabilities of adults range from mild to severe. By the time they are adults, many dyslexics have learned to read. Their problem is not that they cannot or do not read, but rather that reading is still an uncomfortable task for them. Thomas G. West, an author on dyslexia, points out that dyslexics "do not necessarily avoid reading. Some writers have observed that those dyslexics who read extensively and are interested in books are probably misdiagnosed and are not dyslexic at all." West argues, however, that "dyslexics are as interested as anyone in the content of books, even though the process of reading may be extraordinarily difficult for them."[22]

How Is Dyslexia Identified?

Reading difficulties are almost always detected in schools, where most children learn to read. A federal law known as the Individuals with Disabilities Education Act requires school districts to determine a child's specific learning disability and provide that child with a "free and appropriate education." Determining why a child has difficulty reading is not a simple task. According to Frank DeSena, director of special education in the Redondo Beach, California, school district, "Children have difficulty learning to read for a variety of reasons, and the challenge for educators is determining why each child has a problem reading and how that child can best be helped."[23] Some children may have problems with their eyes or ears that can be easily corrected with lenses or hearing aids. Some children may come from homes where English is not spoken or where books are not available. Other children may have behavioral or emotional issues that interfere with learning. Still other children may have the neurological deficits that characterize dyslexia.

Teachers and parents are the people most likely to recognize that a child is having difficulty learning to read. Typically, once a teacher or parent raises a concern, a team of educators in the school will review the child's performance and school records to see if there is an obvious problem with a simple solution. For example, a child who is easily distracted may be helped by moving closer to the teacher. A child who is suspected to be dyslexic, however, needs to be thoroughly evaluated. That process of evaluation is known as an assessment.

Hiding and Compensating for Dyslexia

Some dyslexic students either hide their disability or compensate for it so well that they are not diagnosed with dyslexia for many years. In this excerpt from her essay "Making the Transition," Emily Staats describes how she managed to hide and compensate for her dyslexia until the challenges of college admission tests forced her to seek help:

As an undiagnosed dyslexic, I read so slowly that I began to think that the only explanation for my slowness was that I loved words. I loved them so much it was hard to move away from them and follow them to the end of the sentence. What was really happening is that I couldn't decode, or break down words. I compensated for this weakness by . . . [remembering] what the word looked like. . . . This was a long process and it

What Is an Assessment?

An assessment consists of gathering information about the student through observation, interviews, and tests. Assessments are conducted by teams that may include school nurses, school psychologists, social workers, speech pathologists, and learning disability specialists. School nurses may check the child's hearing and vision and, if necessary, refer him or her to specialists for further evaluation. Social workers may visit the home of the student to gather information about the student's family life. Psychologists may check to see if the child has behavioral conditions such as ADHD.

Once the team has ruled out visual, hearing, behavioral, and social problems, they can focus on intelligence and achievement tests. Standard IQ tests are used to measure the child's intelligence. If a child scores at or above average levels, a learning disability such as dyslexia is more strongly suspected.

slowed me down. It became even more difficult as the words got longer and longer. . . . I hoped not to be noticed or asked to read aloud. . . . [A]lthough I knew that I had reading issues I hid them from everybody and diverted attention by being a wildflower [wallflower] in the back of the classroom. . . .

I couldn't finish reading assignments during class in the time allotted. . . . I became really good at faking that I had read the information by picking out an idea from the reading and asking a question or making a comment about it.

I was diagnosed with dyslexia when I was at the point of complete emotional and physical exhaustion. After 11 years in school, I had grown very tired of hiding my problems from teachers, family and peers. . . . Although I desperately wanted to go to a good college, I wasn't sure how I was going to keep up my elaborate compensation strategies and still succeed. . . . I took the Academic Achievement Test . . . and bombed it. Tired and scared I told my mother my score and many tissue boxes later, we decided to try to find an answer.

A school professional gives a series of assessment tests to a student she suspects suffers from dyslexia. These tests will help her determine an appropriate treatment.

Additional oral and written tests focus specifically on the use of language. These tests are used to determine the student's ability to understand the language and use it appropriately. In oral language tests, students are asked questions to show the level of their phonemic awareness as well as their ability to understand the meaning of words. Students are also asked to read out loud to demonstrate their ability to read correctly and fluently. In written language tests, students' writing samples are reviewed for spelling and correct word usage.

Phonemic Awareness Tests

When dyslexia is suspected, the evaluation team might evaluate a student using several specific tests related to phonemic awareness. One example of a common test is the "pig latin" test. Many children enjoy speaking pig latin, in which they remove the first letter of a word, move it to the end, and then add *ay*. For example, the word *bag* becomes *agbay* in pig latin. When dyslexics are asked to convert a word to its pig latin form, they find it very challenging because of their difficulty in taking apart the sounds in a word.

Dyslexics also have difficulty figuring out what a word would be if one phoneme were to be replaced by another. For example, when asked what word is formed when the sound /b/ in the word *bed* is replaced with the sound /r/, dyslexics are unable to or take a long time to supply the correct answer, *red*. In another test, known as a phoneme deletion test, the task is to figure out what word would remain if a certain sound were removed from it. As an example, when asked what word would remain if the phoneme /pl/ were removed from the word *plant*, dyslexics have difficulty supplying the answer *ant*.

Another test used to analyze a child's phonemic awareness is the nonsense word, or nonword, test. In this type of test, children are asked to decode or sound out nonwords such as *torp, sint, gern, pnir*. According to dyslexia researcher Margaret J. Snowling, "The most direct way of assessing a child's decoding skill is by asking them to read nonwords they have not encountered before."[24] The reason nonword reading is considered the best method for assessing decoding skills is because, regardless of whether someone is dyslexic, nonwords have to be sounded out. In addition, it would not be possible for dyslexics to read nonwords easily by memorizing them or by figuring them out from the context of a sentence. Nonword testing has shown that nondyslexics are usually able to decode these words, even though they have no meaning in English. Dyslexics, on the other hand, have great difficulty in decoding nonwords.

Reading Tests

As part of their assessment, students with reading difficulties are asked to read out loud. Assessment teams listen carefully to detect whether students read correctly and with confidence. One of the important factors in analyzing reading tests is the educational level of the student. A first-grader who mispronounces some words or even transposes letters may not necessarily be dyslexic. Yet a fifth-grader who makes consistent errors and who reads slowly and with obvious difficulty may well be dyslexic.

Even students who correctly, but slowly, sound out words may be considered reading disabled. Sounding out words is part of the process of learning to read and would not be unusual in a first-grader. However, a student in middle or high school who still painfully sounds out words has a reading disability. As Shaywitz states, "A child who reads accurately but not fluently is dyslexic."[25]

Reading Comprehension Tests

Reading involves two processes: the process of identifying the words being read and the process of understanding them. As part of a complete evaluation, assessment teams use reading comprehension tests to help determine whether a student may have a reading disability. In reading comprehension tests, students are asked to read a story or a passage from a book and then answer questions about the passage to determine how well they understand it. Reading comprehension tests are especially important in older students, who may have learned to decode or identify words but who still have difficulty understanding everything they read.

Some dyslexic students score well on reading comprehension tests because they are able to determine the meanings of words from the context in which they are used. Reading comprehension tests by themselves are not good indicators of dyslexia. Combined with phonemic awareness tests, however, they may contribute to a better understanding of why a student has difficulty reading.

Spelling

Spelling tests are also commonly used in dyslexia assessment to determine levels of phonemic awareness. According to Snowling, "One of the very significant and persisting consequences of a phonological processing deficit is a difficulty with spelling."[26] Although many nondyslexic students make errors in spelling, dyslexics make unusual errors that reveal their lack of phonemic awareness. Nondyslexics tend to make errors in spelling that are phonetically acceptable; when the misspelled words are pronounced, they sound the same as the correctly spelled words. For example, misspelling the word *anchor* as *ankur* is phonetically acceptable since both words would be pronounced the same way. Dyslexics, on the other hand, tend to make spelling errors that

are phonetically unacceptable. For example, misspelling the word *laugh* as *lin* indicates that the speller does not recognize the phonemes /l/ /a/ /f/ as the sounds of *laugh*.

Snowling cautions that poor spelling by itself is not a reliable indication of dyslexia. She points out that "cases of people who can read well but who spell poorly highlight that reading and spelling are not identical processes."[27] For example, a person who knows the alphabet and has learned to sound out words may be able to read the word *synchronicity* but not be able to spell it in a spelling test. Along with other test results, spelling tests aid the assessment team in determining whether a student may have the characteristic phonemic deficits that contribute to dyslexia.

Additional Tests

Although language-related tests are the most common ones in diagnosing dyslexia, additional tests may also be used to identify the disorder. These tests include memory tests, tests of visual/spatial skills such as mazes or puzzles, and speed of processing tests in which students are asked to name a letter, number, word, shape, or color as quickly as possible.

A Day in the Life of a Dyslexic

In his book The Secret Life of the Dyslexic Child, *Robert Frank, an educational psychologist and a professor of psychology who is dyslexic, describes how various symptoms of dyslexia mark a typical day in his life.*

Early in the morning, . . . I check my e-mail and usually encounter my first problem of the day. So, I'm up for only 10 minutes before being acutely reminded I'm dyslexic! . . . Once in a while, there will be a note from a reporter asking me to e-mail back the answers to five simple questions or something like that. Not knowing of my dyslexia, the reporter probably assumes this might take me all of 10 minutes. But in reality, such a task might take me several hours. . . .

Today, . . . I have to make sure [my daughter] A.J. takes her medicine for an ear infection. The two of us take great pains to make sure she gets the right amount, reading the directions several times very carefully.

A.J. needs a note for her teacher, explaining in detail why she missed a deadline for a paper. The reason has to do with the ear infection . . . , but it's much too complicated for me to put down on paper. I promise A.J. I will call her teacher. . . . Writing a note in such a hurry about a topic as seemingly simple as this is just too complicated for me. . . .

[Later,] I teach my classes. . . . Once in a while, I'll forget a word when I'm teaching, and I'll call on my students for assistance. . . . My students know I'm dyslexic, so if I forget a word here or there, they call out to help.

While fMRI scans and other brain tests are used by researchers in laboratories, such scans are not used in dyslexia assessments. Although researchers have determined that dyslexics use language processing areas of the brain in different ways than nondyslexics, the technology cannot currently be used as a diagnostic tool. In the future, however, fMRI or similar technology may be used to detect dyslexia in young students. Shaywitz explains:

> This technology has been an extraordinary advance, but I don't want to mislead people. We can't use it yet to diagnose an individual. Someone cannot get into the scanner and say, "Aha, I have an image, and I can have a diagnosis." But I have no doubt about the *potential* for this technology to diagnose people early and more precisely and then to actually examine the effects of interventions.[28]

Diagnosing Adult Dyslexics

Despite the widespread awareness of dyslexia and the methods of assessment among educators, some students are not identified as dyslexic until they are adults in college or at work. Some dyslexic students become adults having spent years frustrated by their reading difficulties and being misunderstood as lazy or dumb. Other dyslexic students make it through school by hiding their disability, compensating for their reading difficulty by working much harder than their peers, and by relying on teachers' oral explanations.

Many adult dyslexics do not realize that they are dyslexic until their children are diagnosed with dyslexia. Dana, for example, realized that she might be dyslexic after her son Brian was diagnosed with the disorder:

> When we found out about Brian's dyslexia, I suddenly realized that I also had the same type of trouble when I was a kid. Not only that, but I realized that my mother also was probably dyslexic. Mom was brilliant, but she didn't like anything that involved reading or writing. I've managed to learn to read, but I wish I'd known then that it wasn't my fault that I had so much trouble reading.[29]

As is true for children, adults have difficulty reading for a variety of reasons. Assessments may be useful for adult dyslexics, even for those who can read but do so poorly, to pinpoint the specific areas in which they most need help. According to Shaywitz:

> While children who are poor readers have not learned the foundational skills, adults, in contrast, may have acquired a smattering of some skills while totally lacking others. And so placement testing is especially important for older disabled readers since each is invariably starting from a different point and typically shows an uneven and unpredictable pattern of reading skills.[30]

For adults who suspect that they might be dyslexic, assessment tests similar to those used by schools are available from private clinics or educational psychologists.

Concerns About Labeling

While assessments are necessary, it is important that assessment teams approach testing with extreme care and caution. Psychol-

Many adults diagnosed with dyslexia are entirely unaware of their disability. Some attribute their reading difficulties to stupidity.

ogists Robert J. Sternberg and Elena L. Grigorenko express the concern that once children are labeled as having a learning disability, "a complex set of mechanisms is put into effect that renders it likely that the label will become a self-fulfilling prophecy, whether it originally was correct or not."[31] For example, a second-grade student may have trouble recognizing English words because she speaks Italian with her family at home. If that student is incorrectly labeled as dyslexic, then she, along with her parents and teachers, may expect reading problems and assume that any trouble she has with reading is caused by a condition she does not actually have.

Some parents who recognize that their children have trouble reading avoid getting them assessed for fear of the stigma of being labeled as dyslexic. Educator Priscilla Vail agrees that labels can be "dangerous when they replace a person's humanity and individuality," but she adds that they are "invaluable when they provide the precise terminology to decide who needs what, when, where, why, and how."[32] Assessment is a necessary first step to getting the right kind of help.

The Importance of Early Detection

Some parents and teachers put off assessing children who have trouble reading. They believe that, given enough time, the children will outgrow their reading difficulties. Studies have shown, however, that children who have dyslexia do not outgrow their reading disability and require diagnosis and appropriate help as early as possible. As Shaywitz states, the belief that reading problems are temporary "is simply not true. Reading problems are not outgrown, they are persistent." Shaywitz adds that research at Yale University has shown that "at least three out of four children who read poorly in third grade continue to have reading problems in high school and beyond."[33]

Getting special instruction before fourth grade can help prevent problems in subjects such as social studies and science in the upper grades. Early detection also helps dyslexic students understand their disability and curbs the frustration that can lead to academic and social failure.

Reading with children can help adults detect symptoms of dyslexia early. Early diagnosis benefits dyslexics in a number of important ways.

The Relief of Diagnosis

A major benefit of diagnosis, regardless of whether the dyslexic is diagnosed as a child or as an adult, is an immense sense of relief in finally understanding the source and nature of the disability. Although dyslexic students and their parents do worry about the impact of dyslexia on their lives, they are relieved to know that the problems in learning to read are not imaginary and are not due to the student's laziness, lack of motivation, or stupidity. Thomas G. West writes that the relief that comes from being diagnosed with dyslexia "should not be underestimated, whether for children or adults, especially for adults. When one has struggled so long without recognition it is a great comfort to have something like objective confirmation of what one has always known but few others believed or understood."[34]

Once dyslexia has been diagnosed, dyslexics and their families can set aside their confusion and worry about the reading disability. With the concerns about laziness or stupidity out of the way, dyslexics can begin to focus on getting effective help.

Chapter 4

Treating Dyslexia

Although dyslexia is a neurological disorder, the primary treatment for it is educational, not medical. Since reading disability is the chief trait in dyslexia, the most common treatment is to give dyslexics special help in learning to read. The process of helping someone overcome reading difficulties is called reading remediation.

Most dyslexic students receive help from the public schools they attend. Help is also available in private schools, after-school clinics, and from private tutors. Some parents choose to send their dyslexic children to residential or boarding schools. Such schools are most appropriate for students with severe dyslexia who might benefit from continuous, intensive help and from being with students with similar learning disabilities.

In schools, dyslexic students usually receive help from special education teachers who have received training in teaching students with learning disabilities. Other professionals who may help dyslexic children and adults include language or speech pathologists, educational psychologists, and specially trained and certified instructors who are experts in a particular reading program.

Individualized Education Program

When a public-school student is identified as dyslexic, a team of the student's parents, teachers, and special education experts prepare a plan of remediation called the individualized education program (IEP). The IEP is a detailed agreement that specifies the educational services and supports to be given to the child with a learning disability. For example, an IEP may specify that a dyslexic student will spend one hour each school day learning to read with a reading specialist and one hour each week with a speech therapist. An IEP can also specify that a particular reading method, such as one that emphasizes phonemic awareness, be used to teach the student.

An IEP typically includes a statement that describes the dyslexic student's current level of performance based on assessment tests. The IEP team then sets specific goals for the student, such as spelling 75 percent of a certain set of words by the end of the semester or being able to read passages in a particular book with 80 percent accuracy by the end of the year. The goals are typically set for the entire school year and will be reviewed at least once during that year.

In preparing an IEP, the IEP team considers a student's strengths as well as weaknesses. For example, a student may have poor handwriting but be very efficient in using a computer keyboard. One of the specific items mentioned in the IEP for such a student

Working with a reading specialist such as this one can help dyslexics to improve their phonemic awareness.

may be that he or she complete all assignments using a word processor.

Teachers and special education experts have general knowledge and experience in helping dyslexic students, but the students' parents can provide valuable and specific information about their dyslexic children. Parents have the right to investigate methods of instruction and make their own recommendations. Students who are fourteen or older are encouraged to participate in preparing the IEP.

Recommended Types of Remediation

Educational laws in the United States require that reading programs used in dyslexia remediation be based on scientific research. In 1997 the U.S. Congress, concerned about the number of children with difficulty learning to read, requested that a panel of experts study available reading methods to determine the most effective methods for teaching children how to read. The panel of experts, known as the National Reading Panel (NRP), reviewed thousands of studies on reading methods and published its results in 2000. The NRP determined that the most successful methods for teaching people how to read were those that emphasized phonemic awareness, the ability to recognize and manipulate sounds within words, and phonics skills, the ability to relate the sounds of speech to the alphabet.

The NRP also determined that all beginning readers benefit from methods that teach phonemic awareness. Phonemic awareness programs consist of tasks such as identifying the common sound in *bat, bird*, and *ball*, identifying the first sound in *pull*, or recognizing the word *ill* when the phoneme /b/ is removed from *bill*. Programs that teach phonemic awareness help prepare beginning readers to understand how sounds are represented by letters and how letters are blended to represent whole words.

The NRP also recommended methods of reading that teach phonics. In phonics instruction, students are explicitly taught the alphabet and its sounds. The panel concluded that "systematic phonics instruction is significantly more effective than non-phonics instruction in helping to prevent reading difficulties among at risk students and in helping to remediate reading difficulties in disabled readers."[35]

There are many programs available to teach beginning readers to read. The NRP found that successful programs emphasize phonemic awareness and phonics, and that multisensory programs are especially helpful to dyslexics.

Multisensory Programs

Multisensory programs use visual, auditory, and tactile means to teach. In such programs, a student who is learning the symbol for the sound /b/, for example, would learn by seeing the letter *b*, hearing and saying the sound it makes, handling a wooden or plastic letter, or tracing the letter in sand or in his or her own palm.

Many multisensory programs are based on the Orton-Gillingham method, developed by Samuel T. Orton, the pioneer dyslexia researcher, and educator Anna Gillingham. In the Orton-Gillingham method, written language is taught systematically, moving from the simple to the more complex. First, the student learns how words can be taken apart into phonemes. Second, the student learns the consonants and vowels that represent single sounds, followed by blended sounds. Third, the student learns about syllables and common roots of words. Fourth, the student learns to master whole words. Finally, the student learns to read whole words within sentences.

Another multisensory program is the Lindamood-Bell program known as the Lindamood Phonemic Sequencing (LiPS) Program. Lindamood-Bell programs are used in clinics as well as in public and private schools. LiPS increases phonemic awareness by making students aware of the lip and tongue motions that produce speech sounds. Students view pictures of people making specific sounds, and they view themselves in mirrors as they make those sounds. Once students are able to separate and manipulate sounds, they are then taught the alphabetical symbols for sounds. When learning the symbols, students see the symbols, hear the sounds they make, and use alphabet tiles to feel the shapes of the letters.

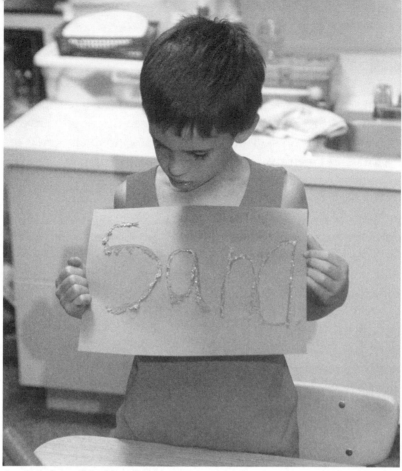

As part of a multisensory-learning program, a boy has written the word sand *with actual sand and glue on a piece of paper.*

Computer-Based Programs

In recent years many reading programs have been adapted for use on computers. One computer-based reading program is Fast ForWord, which contains a series of reading remediation programs for children of various reading abilities—those who have not yet learned to read, beginning readers, and middle and high school students who have difficulty reading. With the Fast ForWord program, students use headphones to listen to instruction and answer questions by clicking the computer mouse. For example in one exercise for children who have not yet learned to read, students hear the word *boy* through the headphones while pictures of a boy and a toy are displayed on the computer screen. The student then uses the mouse to click on the correct matching picture. For beginning readers, Fast ForWord offers exercises in which students learn to identify phonemes and relate sounds to letters. Middle and high school students can develop their reading comprehension skills through exercises in which they listen to stories and then answer questions that test their ability to identify details in the stories.

Teachers or parents who use Fast ForWord can track the progress of their students by linking to the manufacturer of the program through the Internet. The progress reports show how well the student has done on each assignment and the specific skill areas that may need additional improvement.

Reading Remediation for Adults

Reading remediation methods that work best for adult dyslexics are the same multisensory and systematic methods that work well for children. While the basics of teaching reading remain the same for children and adults, reading programs become much more effective for adults when they are adapted to their needs. For example, a reading program known as Language! identifies the reader's level of reading and can link the

This student uses a computerized educational program. Computer programs exist to assist dyslexic students at all grade levels.

reader to thousands of books categorized by his or her level of difficulty. These books are sorted by topics such as sports, history, science, and mystery, and readers can choose the books appropriate for their reading level in those topics.

Throughout the United States, programs are available to help improve reading skills of adults. These programs, known as adult literacy programs, are typically available through adult schools and public libraries. In recent years employers and labor unions have offered special reading programs customized to their workplaces. A reading program for plumbers, for instance, might contain chapters on pipe repair and unclogging sinks. According to Sally E. Shaywitz, participation in such customized programs can be very effective and "highly motivating; for example, instruction focused on the most common words in work-related materials can allow a worker to function more easily at his job or help him move on to the next level."[36]

Assistive Technologies

In addition to remediation programs, technologies are available to assist dyslexics with reading and writing. These differ from remediation programs in that they do not teach dyslexics how to read. Instead they make reading and writing simpler for dyslexics. These technologies, known as assistive technologies, include word-processing, voice-recognition, and text-to-speech systems.

Assistive technologies are especially helpful for students who are able to decode words but still have difficulty with fluency and spelling. Without assistive technologies, older dyslexic students may find it difficult to keep up with the increasing demands of reading history textbooks or writing essays for literature classes.

Word Processing

Word processing is one of the most common and helpful assistive technologies. For many dyslexics, using a keyboard to type in letters is physically easier than handwriting. According to Joanne Lande, a special education teacher who is an expert in assistive technologies, "One of the big advantages of using a keyboard is that each letter becomes associated with a location on the keyboard. So someone who might write the letter *b* as a *d* is much less likely to make the same mistake on the keyboard, because he or she remembers a location on the keyboard instead of remembering if the loop goes on the left or right of the line."[37]

Some dyslexics have illegible handwriting because they awkwardly grip their pencils. Teachers reading poorly handwritten assignments might not be able to make out what dyslexic students have written and might mark answers wrong even though they are correct. For both dyslexics and their teachers, then, the use of word processors can be very helpful.

Another major benefit of word processors is that they usually have a spell-checking feature that allows the students to check and correct any spelling errors. Some word processors have a word-prediction feature that anticipates a word based on the first few letters typed. For example, a student who wants to type the word *benefit* needs to only key in the letters *ben-* for the word processor to predict that the word to be typed is *benefit* and automatically fill in the letters *-efit* to complete the word.

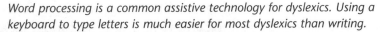

Word processing is a common assistive technology for dyslexics. Using a keyboard to type letters is much easier for most dyslexics than writing.

Voice-Recognition Programs

Voice-recognition software can also be very helpful for dyslexics. Voice-recognition programs such as Dragon NaturallySpeaking allow users to say what they want to write into a microphone. The program automatically types the spoken words into a word-processing file that can be spell-checked and printed. Another useful feature is that the program can read out loud the document it has processed. This feature allows dyslexics to hear their document, in addition to seeing it, and allows them to make corrections if necessary. Voice-recognition software can be especially helpful for older dyslexic students and adults who need to write long school essays or frequently need to communicate in writing.

Text-to-Speech Programs

Text-to-speech programs that convert written words into spoken words are another form of assistive technology. An example of this type of technology is the Kurzweil reading system. This system uses a computer and a scanner to help dyslexics read. A student who needs to read a chapter in a history book, for instance, can scan the chapter into the computer. The Kurzweil system then displays the chapter on the computer screen. When the student instructs the program to begin reading, a portion of the text (a line, a sentence, or a paragraph, as desired by the student) is highlighted on the screen. As the system begins to read out loud, each word it reads is highlighted by a different color in the background.

A student using the Kurzweil system can slow down or speed up its reading pace. The system has many other functions, such as pronouncing highlighted words, breaking words into syllables, or giving their definitions and synonyms. In addition to reading documents that are scanned in, the Kurzweil system can be used to read the student's own word-processed documents as well as e-mail and Web pages on the Internet.

Another text-to-speech tool is the Reading Pen. Dyslexics use this portable reading tool much like they would a highlighter pen. As the reader points the Reading Pen at the line to be read, the pen scans in the words, reads them aloud, and defines them.

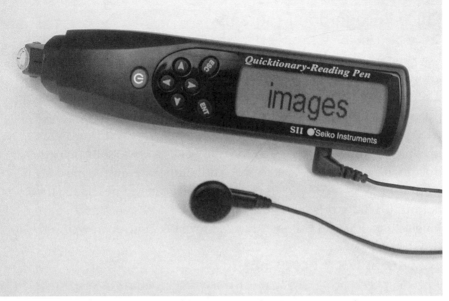

The Reading Pen is a portable scanner and text-to-voice machine. Drawn over words like a highlighter, the pen scans, reads aloud, and defines words in a line of text.

Factors in Successful Remediation

In addition to selecting appropriate programs for remediation—those that emphasize phonemic awareness and phonics—there are other factors that contribute to successful remediation. These factors include the intensity and frequency of help, the age of the student, the severity of the disability, and the quality of the instructor.

Studies have shown that dyslexic students improve their reading skills more quickly when they receive frequent and intense one-on-one attention. Getting individual attention is highly effective because the teacher can focus on the student's specific problems, and the student is not distracted by classmates. Special education expert Frank DeSena comments that "one-on-one attention is so effective that special education programs could almost be eliminated if all students were in small classrooms of four or five students where teachers could give them individualized attention."[38] School districts have limited budgets, however, and ideal one-on-one settings, or even small group settings, are rarely achieved.

Dyslexic children have a greater likelihood of responding favorably to remediation if dyslexia is detected early. According to dyslexia expert Susan Hall, "The ideal window for addressing reading difficulties is during kindergarten and first grade." Hall adds that "while it is still possible to help an older child with reading, those beyond third grade require much more intensive help."[39]

The effectiveness of remediation also depends on the severity of the reading disability. No two dyslexics respond in the same way to remediation because the severity of reading disability

A grandfather helps his dyslexic granddaughter use a scanner for a reading program. Such intimate attention can help dyslexics overcome their disabilities.

ranges from very slight to very serious. Whereas students with mild cases of dyslexia respond more easily and quickly to remediation, those with a more severe disability take longer to improve. Dyslexics who also have other disabilities, such as ADHD, have greater challenges to overcome and take longer to improve.

The quality of the instructor is another important factor in remediation. Teaching dyslexics to read is demanding work. It requires sensitivity, tolerance, persistence, and mastery of effective programs. As educator Louisa Moats says, "Teaching reading *is* rocket science."[40] Special education teachers need to be flexible and try multiple teaching methods until they find the style most suitable for each individual dyslexic student.

Challenges in Remediation

While educators recognize and attempt to achieve the factors that make for successful remediation, several issues pose challenges in remediation. A major concern in education for dyslexics is with the concept of discrepancy, the idea that there must be a gap between a child's ability (as measured by IQ tests) and achievement (as measured by reading scores) before a child can be identified as dyslexic and receive help in public schools. Educator Sheldon H. Horowitz writes that relying on the discrepancy model "virtually requires that students 'crash and burn' academically before they can gain access to special education services and it reinforces failure, ultimately making remediation much more difficult."[41] Many experts recommend that all children who have difficulty reading be offered help regardless of whether a discrepancy between their ability and achievement exists.

Another concern for educators is that the Individuals with Disabilities Education Act requires that students receive special education in the least restrictive environment. To comply with the requirement, students with learning disabilities are "mainstreamed," which means that they are placed in regular classrooms rather than in special education ones. In a regular classroom, however, dyslexic students do not receive the intense, individualized help that works best for them and that can only be found in very small groups or in one-on-one settings.

Results of Remediation

Educational researchers regularly study the effectiveness of various remediation programs. In 2003 a research team at Stanford University demonstrated for the first time that effective remediation not only improves reading skills but also changes brain function in dyslexics. The Stanford researchers performed various phonological tests and fMRI scans on twenty dyslexic students both before and after an intensive remediation program (the Fast ForWord program for beginning readers). At the end of the remediation study, the phonological tests showed that the dyslexic students had improved significantly in reading. In addition, the fMRI scans showed that, after remediation, the dyslexics' brain functions in the language processing centers had become more like those of nondyslexic readers. More studies are necessary to determine what aspects of Fast ForWord and other programs are specifically responsible for changing brain function in dyslexics.

Alternative Therapies

For the vast majority of dyslexics, overcoming their disorder requires extensive reading remediation. A minority of dyslexics may also be helped by a few alternative therapies. Most researchers believe that these therapies alone will not help dyslexics, but for some, they may be helpful in addition to reading remediation. Available alternative therapies include movement or balance therapies, visual therapies, and nutritional therapies.

Movement therapies are based on the cerebellar theory that relates dyslexia to a dysfunction in the brain that interferes with motor skill development. These therapies provide exercise programs that are intended to develop and improve balance and coordination. Movement therapists believe that the exercises retrain neural pathways to deal more efficiently with reading.

Visual therapies are based on the theory that dyslexics have impaired visual processing. One therapy program recommends that dyslexics cover one eye with a patch when reading. According to John Stein and Joel Talcott, covering one eye stabilizes dyslexics' vision and "eliminates fluctuating double vision, which is one potent cause of their tendency to merge and transpose

Practice, Practice, Practice

In this excerpt from her book To Read or Not to Read, *reading specialist Daphne M. Hurford describes how one of her students, Cyp, learned to read by working hard and by "overlearning," or practicing each lesson over and over until he mastered it.*

In the beginning, everything was a struggle for Cyp; nothing made sense or came easily. Hundreds of three- by five-inch index cards later, he had learned the consonant sounds and how to write them. . . . Cyp learned that there were such things as short vowel sounds, and he . . . created pictures representing them. Index cards . . . were lined up at his side every session, all session, so that he could always consult them, to see and say the word and to visually remind himself of the particular sound/symbol relationship he was seeking. Then he learned to sequence the consonant and vowel sounds into words, left to right. This is often a serious sticking point for dyslexics, but with a lot of work, Cyp learned how to do it. Next he discovered that *pl* and *gr* and *tw* and *sn* . . . blend their sounds together. . . . After that he found out that sometimes vowels appear together. . . .

Enormous effort went into mastering all of this information. . . . Step by step, building block by building block, Cyp learned

letters."[42] To be effective, Stein and Talcott caution that the patch method should be used in children who are between six and nine years of age in order to take advantage of what Stein and Talcott consider to be the ideal developmental stage for visual therapy.

Another visual therapy is known as the Irlen method, in which an assortment of aids, such as color-tinted lenses and visors for

to read, to become reasonably fluent, and to understand what he was reading. . . . It was all done slowly, incrementally, multisensorily, and everything was repeated and repeated so that he could "overlearn" it. That is another important concept, overlearning. Dyslexic students can't be taught something once and be expected to have learned it and to remember it. Their memories are not so reliable, particularly for words and sounds, so they have to be taught and retaught until they show they have mastered what they are learning. They need to practice, practice, practice, and then practice again.

Repetition is an important learning tool for dyslexics, who can learn to write by practicing the skill over and over.

reducing glare, are used to make the reading experience easier for dyslexics who report visual complaints such as words shimmering or disappearing from the page. Many dyslexia experts believe that color lenses are only helpful to a small minority of dyslexics. According to John J. Ratey, "It's important to note that Irlen lenses help with only a small fraction of people who suffer from dyslexia."[43]

Nutritional therapies for dyslexia involve supplements such as omega-3 fatty acids, which are found in fish. Supporters of nutritional therapy believe that increasing the amount of fatty acid consumed either through supplements or through diet helps correct visual and brain function. The research in nutritional therapy has been limited, and the evidence that dyslexics may benefit from nutritional therapies is slim.

Potential Future Treatments

Since dyslexia is a neurological disorder, it is possible that in the future scientists will be able to devise treatments that work directly on the neurological impairments. One possibility is that scientists might be able to manufacture drugs that can offset the effects of impairments in language processing centers or in magnocells. Drug therapies are currently available for a number of neurological disorders, such as depression and Alzheimer's disease, and research is under way to develop drugs for many more brain-based disorders. Dyslexia may well be another disorder for which drug therapy will be available in the future.

Scientists are currently working to identify the gene or genes that lead to dyslexia. In the future it may be possible for scientists to study children's genes and then identify those children who are at risk for dyslexia. By identifying dyslexic children soon after birth, early steps can be taken to prevent reading disabilities. Another possible, though much less likely, application of genetic research may be gene therapy, a controversial and experimental procedure used to repair or replace defective genes. Currently, gene therapy carries significant risks, and it is not anticipated that it will be used in treating learning disabilities in the near future.

In the meantime, the most effective treatment remains reading remediation. Although alternative therapies may be useful as a treatment in addition to remediation, very few dyslexics improve without getting intense, frequent, multisensory instruction that emphasizes phonemic awareness and phonics. Once dyslexics do learn to read, they need to learn to cope with their disability, which poses lifelong challenges.

Chapter 5

Living and Coping with Dyslexia

The effects of dyslexia extend far beyond the classroom. While dyslexia is a disability specific to language, it has broader psychological and social effects that impact the lives of dyslexic children, their parents, and their siblings. The period of time before being diagnosed may be particularly stressful since dyslexics do not understand the cause of their difficulty. Yet even after being diagnosed and receiving appropriate help, dyslexics need to learn to cope with their lifelong condition.

Despite the challenges posed by dyslexia, it is possible for dyslexics and their families to successfully adjust to the disorder. In addition to reading programs aimed at their phonemic deficits, dyslexics benefit from modified classroom requirements, getting emotional support from their families, and by tapping into their strengths and talents. The path to successful adjustment is not easy; dyslexics and their families must deal with a range of difficulties, including frustration, embarrassment, anxiety, lack of self-esteem, and other psychological issues.

Frustration and Embarrassment

The most common feelings that dyslexics experience are frustration and embarrassment. Just having difficulty in reading is by itself very frustrating, but what dyslexics find even more frustrating and embarrassing is that they have difficulty doing something that most of their classmates seem to find easy. To make things worse, many people assume that dyslexics have trouble reading because they do not try hard enough. The mistaken perceptions of people

Dyslexic students often experience frustration and embarrassment as a result of their learning difficulties. Such frustration can lead to serious psychological problems.

around them cause dyslexics a great deal of emotional pain. As author Thomas G. West writes, "To have extreme difficulty with things that are easy for one's peers is painful. To be told that one's problems result merely from laziness or lack of motivation is difficult to bear."[44]

Dyslexic students may be especially embarrassed when they are asked to read aloud in class or answer questions. One dyslexic college student remembers his feelings of embarrassment: "It was really scary in class when I had to read out loud. I'd start to cough, stumble and just try to get the words out as quickly as possible."[45] Although most teachers and some classmates now understand learning disabilities, those who do not may cause dyslexics extreme embarrassment. Robert Frank, an educational psychologist who is dyslexic, remembers being called "stupid" by a teacher in front of his classmates when he could not answer a question:

I remember sitting in the back of the class, with all the other children turned to look at me, as she accused me of being stupid. This was a traumatic experience that I will never forget. While I can no longer recall the exact question she asked, the feeling of embarrassment and frustration I felt at that moment is indelibly etched in my memory.[46]

Low Self-Esteem and Anxiety

Along with feeling frustrated and embarrassed about how other people see them, dyslexics frequently blame themselves for their difficulties. The combination of these feelings leads many dyslexics to develop poor self-images. They suspect they might be stupid, and they lose their confidence in trying to learn new things. Even dyslexics who are aware that they are intelligent might doubt themselves and consider themselves failures. A dyslexic college student enrolled in a doctoral program remembers how she felt as a child:

Teasing, crying and self-loathing were daily events in grade school. I considered myself the proverbial "dumb kid." Being intelligent, bright, and dyslexic was extremely frustrating. I knew I was as smart or smarter than the other kids, but I couldn't show that. . . . I couldn't understand why I was so different. I hated myself for being a failure. Temper tantrums weren't uncommon. I couldn't escape from the despair and disgust.[47]

Dyslexic children often worry that their classmates might find out about their problem and not accept them. According to Frank, dyslexics live in fear, "a fear that afflicts all children at one time or another—the fear of not fitting in."[48] In order to keep their disability a secret, some dyslexic students may avoid situations in which their disability might become apparent. Frank describes several ways that dyslexic children may attempt to hide their disability, such as "shying away from the drama club, skipping a day of school or feigning illness when there's a spelling test, and walking off the playground when the kids who are jumping rope start reciting rhymes."[49]

Pressure to Perform

Dyslexic students, especially those who have not been diagnosed, often feel a great deal of pressure to do well in school. A graduate nursing student describes how she felt:

High school was the most difficult for me. I didn't know I had dyslexia. I just thought I was stupid. My grades didn't meet my parents' expectations. They criticized me for not doing my homework, even though I studied for hours without accomplishing much. I think my teachers would have been more supportive if I'd opened up to them, but I felt so much shame.[50]

The pressure to do well in school may be especially high for dyslexic students who have older nondyslexic siblings. Parents and teachers who are familiar with the older child's academic skills may have expectations for the dyslexic sibling based on their experience with the older child. Anne describes the pressure her younger dyslexic brother John felt: "John felt pressured to be an 'A' student because we went to the same K-8 school and all the teachers expected him to be like me. But he wasn't. He had dyslexia."[51]

Fatigue

Dyslexic children get fatigued more easily than nondyslexic ones because they need to work harder. Frank explains that "everything takes longer for the dyslexic child: writing, spelling, reading, following directions, studying. . . . A simple task like looking up a number in a phone book can become an aggravating chore for a dyslexic child or adult."[52]

Researchers at the University of Washington have discovered one reason why dyslexics get so easily fatigued. Brain imaging scans have shown that dyslexic children use nearly five times the brain area that nondyslexic children use when performing language tasks. According to researcher Todd Richards, "This means their brains were working a lot harder and using more energy than the normal children." Fellow researcher Virginia Berninger adds, "People often don't see how hard it is for dyslexic children to do a task that others do so effortlessly."[53]

Troubled Dyslexics

Dyslexics sometimes feel isolated and find it difficult to make friends. It is difficult for children who are teased by their classmates to form relationships with peers outside of the classroom. Some dyslexics become angry and disruptive, and others try to be the class clown. Frank DeSena, a special education director, explains: "Some children with learning disabilities prefer to be thought of as disruptive or as clowns instead of as learning disabled. They feel that acting out makes them more acceptable to their peers, when having a learning disability wouldn't."[54]

Some dyslexics, especially those who do not receive appropriate help, become so frustrated with their learning disability that they begin to avoid school, eventually dropping out before completing their education. Dyslexics who drop out are less likely to find rewarding work and are more likely to engage in antisocial behavior or even crime. According to the National Center for Education Statistics, more than one-third of prisoners in the United States have a learning disability and more than two-thirds of them either cannot read or have limited reading skills. Educator Priscilla Vail explains that when students "are only recognized for their inadequacies, they may turn against themselves, schooling, or society in general." Vail continues:

> An uncomfortable truth, revealed in countless research studies, is that correctional institutions, juvenile and adult, are filled with inmates who are imprisoned by their illiteracy as well as the bars on their cells and buildings. These are the different

A girl falls asleep while reading. Dyslexics exert much more energy than nondyslexics on tasks like reading and writing.

Dyslexia and Delinquency

The observation that illiteracy is common in prisons has led researchers to investigate more closely the prevalence of dyslexia among delinquents and prisoners. Since illiteracy may be due to factors other than dyslexia—factors such as inadequate instruction or behavioral disorders—researchers have begun to assess the phonemic awareness and decoding skills of prisoners.

In June 2004 the British Dyslexia Association (BDA) released the results of a study of thirty-four teenage delinquents in their report entitled "Unrecognised Dyslexia and the Route to Offending." The researchers found that nineteen of the delinquents (or 56 percent of the group) displayed symptoms of dyslexia. The BDA study also made reference to several other studies that show a high incidence of dyslexia among in-

learners who turned their energies into attacks on a system that gave neither help nor support.[55]

Parents of Dyslexics

Next to dyslexics themselves, the people most likely to be affected by dyslexia are parents of dyslexic children. For parents, the diagnosis of dyslexia can trigger a range of emotions. Some parents attempt to deny the problem and seek to blame the child's teachers or instructional methods. Other parents feel tremendous guilt, blaming themselves for being inadequate parents. For example, some parents wonder if they should spend more time with their children, help them more with their homework, or if they should have read more often to them when they were younger. Some parents who are themselves dyslexic, or had known that dyslexia was present in their family, feel guilty about having passed on dyslexic tendencies to their children.

mates. In one study, completed in 1997, researchers discovered that 31 percent of inmates in a Swedish prison had significant difficulty in decoding words and in comprehension. Another Swedish study of teenage delinquents showed that 70 percent of the teenagers in the group had difficulty reading, and 11 percent of them specifically had phonological difficulties. In a 1999 study of young offenders in Scotland, 50 percent of the group were identified as having some indications of dyslexia, and 12 percent were identified as having strong indications of dyslexia.

The BDA report also identifies a "route to offending," a path that leads young people to criminal behavior. According to the BDA report, the route to offending "starts with difficulties in the classroom, moves through low self-esteem, poor behaviour and school exclusion, and ends in offending. Children and young people with dyslexia are more likely to fall onto this route, because of the difficulties they face with learning."

Some parents are very alarmed by the diagnosis of dyslexia in their children. This is especially true for parents who excelled in school and assumed that their children would also be strong academic performers. One parent describes how she and her husband, Jason, reacted when they discovered their daughter Brenda had dyslexia:

> Both Jason and I were highly academic students, so it was difficult to see Brenda struggling in school. Everything came easy to us. When Brenda was first diagnosed, we were in shock. I didn't know about dyslexia. I didn't know about learning disabilities. All I knew was we were going to have these perfect children. We'd had an easy life so far. When we got the test results, we panicked. . . . The thought of what could be in store for Brenda, and us, was horrifying.[56]

Although some parents respond to their child's dyslexia by disappointment and even anger toward their child, for many parents the diagnosis can trigger a surge of protective feelings. These parents try to learn everything they can about dyslexia and may become strong advocates for their children. One parent describes how she responded when she found out her son Dylan had dyslexia: "I'd heard of dyslexia, but I really didn't know much about it. When Dylan was diagnosed, I checked out from the library every book on dyslexia I could find. I must have read twenty books on it."[57] Another parent was extremely moved by watching her son Charles struggle with dyslexia: "My heart goes out to our son. . . . He struggles to keep up with his peers. . . . Charles always has struggled with being different. I don't believe he's felt like his peers. Yet, he wants so much to be like every other child. To me, he's a hero."[58]

Siblings of Dyslexics

Dyslexia impacts the siblings of dyslexics as well. Many siblings feel responsible for taking care of their dyslexic brothers or sisters. Even when the nondyslexic sibling is younger than the dyslexic sibling, he or she may feel protective and responsible for the older dyslexic sibling. This places a significant burden on the nondyslexic sibling, who, in addition to worrying about himself or herself, worries about the dyslexic sibling's well-being. Rachel, for example, feels very protective toward her sister Sarah:

> When we were much younger, I was like Sarah's mother. I protected her. I did everything for her. We had a very close bond. As an infant, Sarah took a while to speak. Her speech wasn't very clear, but I could understand her. I would tell mom what Sarah was saying. . . .
>
> I still want to protect Sarah. She gets teased a lot at school.[59]

In some families, nondyslexic siblings feel pressured to perform well in school to make up for the disappointment some parents feel about the academic performance of their dyslexic children. Nondyslexic siblings frequently feel that the efforts they make are not as appreciated as the efforts made by their dyslexic siblings. Penelope, for example, remembers how differently her mother viewed Penelope's and her sister Maureen's similar grades: "What I never really understood was that it was OK for Maureen to get 'B's,' but not me. I guess my mom sensed I was better than 'B's.' And in helping Maureen so much, she realized 'B's' for Maureen were like 'A's' for me. But to an elementary-school kid, it was hard to comprehend."[60]

Some siblings also feel that their accomplishments are disregarded while the similar or less stellar performance of the dyslexic child is praised. Melinda, for example, noticed that once her sister Robin was diagnosed with dyslexia, "my parents made a big deal out of any 'A' Robin got, but the fact that I'd been getting practically straight 'A's' for years was taken for granted."[61]

The siblings of dyslexics often feel personally responsible for the well-being of their dyslexic brothers or sisters.

Some siblings come to resent the extra attention their dyslexic siblings get from their parents and families. They feel that their concerns and problems are ignored while the dyslexic child's problems become the focus of the family. Nicki, a thirteen-year-old in eighth grade, describes how her brother Taylor's dyslexia impacts her: "In some ways I wish Taylor did not have a learning disability because it would be easier for me, for selfish reasons. He gets a lot of attention from my parents and our baby-sitter. I need attention, too—I'm a teenager and I have a lot of questions. Mom tries to make special time with me, but it doesn't happen that often."[62]

Dyslexic Adults

Dyslexic adults share many of the same feelings as dyslexic children. By the time dyslexics reach adulthood they have struggled for many years with their disability. For adults whose dyslexia was never identified, their frustration with their difficulty may be compounded by additional emotions such as anger and depression. Adult dyslexics who have not received help are likely to lack confidence and have low self-esteem.

Some dyslexic adults try to minimize their discomfort by avoiding reading. It is difficult, however, to go through life in a literate society without having to read at times. Adults have to be able to read to pay bills, to know which exit to take off a highway, or to know how to take medicines. Adults whose reading skills are limited may have the burden of trying to provide for themselves and their families with low-paying jobs. For adults who have not been diagnosed and helped, dyslexia is a disability that interferes with the quality of their everyday lives.

Successful Adjustments

Although dyslexics and their families are greatly challenged by dyslexia, it is possible for them to accept the condition and make successful adjustments. In addition to reading remediation, success for dyslexics may depend on three critical elements: emotional support, classroom or workplace accommodations, and discovering their strengths and talents.

Emotional Support

It is crucial that dyslexics have family, friends, or teachers who provide them with encouragement. For many dyslexic children, their parents are the most influential people in supporting and guiding them. One dyslexic college student describes how her parents' support helped her cope with her dyslexia: "My family support also was a key factor. My father recorded textbook assignments for me on tape. My mother encouraged me to be my own person and to explore all of my creative options. . . . Knowing someone believed in me was very energizing. It reminded me there wasn't anything I couldn't handle."[63]

An area in which dyslexic children need a great deal of help is with self-esteem. Robert Frank explains:

> For the dyslexic child, self-esteem is an especially sensitive area because many dyslexic kids are treated as if they are not "smart," particularly by those who do not understand the nature of the disability. . . . A child who feels the unconditional love of his family and friends is more likely to feel good about himself than one who feels he is loved or accepted only when he lives up to certain standards or behaviors.[64]

Classroom Accommodations

Dyslexics are also helped when teachers make changes to some of their requirements. These changes are known as accommodations. The single most important accommodation for dyslexics is being given more time to take tests and complete assignments. Without additional time, a dyslexic student taking a history test, for example, may not be able to answer all the questions in time simply because it takes him or her longer to read them.

Other accommodations include allowing dyslexic students to tape lectures and giving them opportunities for extra-credit assignments. A dyslexic student assigned to read a novel can be encouraged to create his or her own multisensory experiences by listening to an audio recording of the book or watching a film, if available. Dyslexic students may also be graded based on their individualized education program objectives and on the

Are Accommodations Unfair?

Some people question the fairness of accommodations. They question, for example, why dyslexics should be allowed extra time to complete tests when nondyslexics are not given extra time. Advocates for dyslexics point out that, without the extra time, dyslexic children do not have an equal opportunity to demonstrate their mastery of a subject. As Sally E. Shaywitz writes in her book *Overcoming Dyslexia*, "Dyslexia robs a person of time; accommodations return it."

One way to make accommodations fair is to make sure the accommodation does not assist the dyslexic to such a degree that the test becomes pointless. For example, allowing a spell-checker during a history exam may be fine, but allowing a spell-checker during a spelling test makes the test meaningless. Mel Levine, a pediatrician who specializes in learning disorders, has another suggestion, which he refers to as payback. Levine writes in his book *A Mind at a Time*, "I often think it's a good idea to ask a child for a payback for accommoda-

improvement they make, as opposed to being graded in comparison to their classmates.

Workplace Accommodations

For adult dyslexics, employers can make accommodations in the workplace to help their employees. For example, checkout procedures in a grocery store can be recorded so dyslexic clerks can listen to instructions instead of reading them. Assistive technologies such as word-processing, voice-recognition, and text-to-speech systems are also very helpful for dyslexics at work. In some cases, these technologies can be modified to meet the specific needs of the workplace. For example, dyslex-

tion, in which case the student may take on some form of additional work to compensate for a reduction of demands in an area of difficulty." For example, Levine suggests telling a student who has been given extra time to turn in a paper, "You are so splendid at art that I would like you to repay me for the accommodation by creating a poster we can hang in the front of the room." Levine explains that the payback system helps students sustain their pride, and is fair to the others for whom no accommodation was made.

Dyslexic students are often given more time than their peers to complete assignments.

ics working in the medical field can modify voice-recognition systems by adding special medical terminology, such as *ankylosing spondylitis* (which refers to a type of inflammation of joints), so the system recognizes and correctly spells those terms when they are spoken. Computers and automated systems can also be modified so that they operate with voice instruction.

Strengths of Dyslexics
Another helpful factor in successful adjustment for dyslexics is the discovery of their talents and strengths. Discovering something they enjoy and excel in helps them see themselves as

worthwhile and valuable people who happen to have a specific difficulty in reading. For Beth, finding her talent felt like coming home: "I finally found the key to set me free. It was long, delicate and silver. It was the flute. As soon as the silver mouthpiece touched my lips, I was home. I had found a way to express myself. Finally my intellect and creativity were out in the open. Finally I could be proud of myself."[65]

Research has shown that while dyslexics have difficulty with language, many of them have strong visual and spatial abilities. Some dyslexic children grow up to be gifted scientists, mathematicians, engineers, and artists. In a study described by psychologist Ellen Winner, a researcher found that children who began speaking later than their peers "tended to have high spatial abilities—they excelled at puzzles, for instance—and most had relatives working in professions that require strong spatial skills."[66]

Winner describes a second study in which a group of college art students made "significantly more spelling errors than college students majoring either in math or in verbal areas such as English or history." Although these students excelled in art, their

---

Dyslexics who develop their innate talents, such as musical ability, typically have an improved sense of self-worth.

ability to spell, and specifically their ability to spell phonetically, was limited. Winner states that "association between verbal deficits and spatial gifts seems particularly strong among visual artists."[67]

In a third study described by Winner, six out of twenty top mathematicians reported having had trouble learning to read. Winner adds that while many academically gifted students learn how to read before attending school, none of the twenty mathematicians had.

The studies described by Winner indicate that some people may be very talented in certain areas—spatial ability, art, mathematics—but still be lacking in verbal ability in comparison to others. It may be difficult for dyslexics and the people around them to believe that someone with a reading disability may be gifted in other areas. There is no contradiction, however, in someone being both gifted and disabled. Dyslexics have a specific difficulty with language, but that difficulty does not keep them from excelling in nonverbal areas. According to Winner, "many children exhibit gifts in one area of study and are unremarkable or even learning disabled in others. These may be creative children who are difficult in school and who are not immediately recognized as gifted."[68]

Dyslexia: A Gift in Disguise?

Whereas some researchers find no contradiction in being reading disabled and gifted, others suggest that dyslexia may be a gift disguised as a problem. Thomas G. West lists the names of many famous and accomplished people who had difficulty with language—including Thomas Edison, Albert Einstein, and Leonardo da Vinci—and argues that "many of these individuals may have achieved success not in spite of but because of their apparent disabilities."[69] To support his argument, West relies on the theory that the two hemispheres of the human brain specialize in different abilities. According to this theory, the left hemisphere is the home of language processing centers, and the right hemisphere is associated with processing visual images, patterns, and spatial relations. West argues that people such as Edison, Einstein,

and da Vinci "may have been so much in touch with their visual-spatial, nonverbal, right-hemisphere modes of thought that they have had difficulty in doing orderly, sequential, verbal-mathematical left-hemisphere tasks."[70]

Whether dyslexia is seen as a gift or a disability depends partly on the society in which dyslexics live. Societies differ greatly in how they view certain human attributes. In modern societies, and particularly in academic settings, the ability to read fluently is highly desirable. Four hundred years ago, when very few people read, someone who was skilled at weaving cloth, farming land, or shooting an arrow would have been valued. Psychologists Robert J. Sternberg and Elena L. Grigorenko believe that "where and when a child is born has a tremendous impact on whether that child will be labeled as having a learning disability. . . . In a preliterate society for example, no children are labeled as having a reading disability. One society might label someone with minimal musical skills as having a musical disability, whereas another society might not."[71]

Viewing dyslexia as a gift does not mean pretending that dyslexics do not have disabilities. Looking at the positive aspects of dyslexia is part of making a successful adjustment to it. Robert Frank writes, "I'd certainly like to live my life without dyslexia," but since he cannot, he prefers to "take to heart the old axiom 'When you're given lemons, make lemonade.'"[7]

Notes

Introduction: A Reading and Learning Disability

1. Brian, interview by author, Redondo Beach, CA, December 3, 2003. (Name changed to respect interviewee's privacy)
2. Dana, interview by author, Redondo Beach, CA, December 3, 2003. (Name changed to respect interviewee's privacy)
3. Sally E. Shaywitz, *Overcoming Dyslexia: A New and Complete Science-Based Program for Overcoming Reading Problems at Any Level.* New York: Knopf, 2003, p. 3.
4. Dana, interview.
5. Shaywitz, *Overcoming Dyslexia*, p. 89.

Chapter 1: The Nature of Dyslexia

6. G. Reid Lyon, "Why Johnny Can't Decode," *Washington Post*, October 27, 1996. www.ldonline.org/ld_indepth/reading/why_johnny_cant_decode.html.
7. Quoted in Shirley Kurnoff, *The Human Side of Dyslexia*. Monterey, CA: London Universal, 2001, pp. 105–106.
8. Quoted in Kurnoff, *The Human Side of Dyslexia*, p. 52.
9. G. Reid Lyon, "Why Reading Is Not a Natural Process," *Learning Disabilities Association of America*, January/February 2000. www.ldonline.org/ld_indepth/reading/why_reading_is_not.html.

Chapter 2: Theories of Dyslexia

10. Quoted in Shaywitz, *Overcoming Dyslexia*, p. 13.
11. Shaywitz, *Overcoming Dyslexia*, p. 78.
12. Shaywitz, *Overcoming Dyslexia*, p. 81.
13. Quoted in Marcia D'Arcangelo, "Learning About Learning to Read: A Conversation with Sally Shaywitz," *Educational*

Leadership, October 1999. www.ascd.org/publications/ed_lead/199910/darcangelo.html.

14. Margaret J. Snowling, *Dyslexia*, 2nd ed. Oxford, UK: Blackwell, 2000, p. 137.

15. Franck Ramus, "The Neural Basis of Reading Acquisition," in (Ed.), *The New Cognitive Neurosciences*, ed. M.S. Gazzaniga, 3rd ed., Cambridge, MA: MIT Press. www.ehess.fr/centres/lscp/persons/ramus/TCNS3.pdf.

16. John Stein and Vincent Walsh, "To See but Not to Read: The Magnocellular Theory of Dyslexia," *Trends in Neuroscience*, November 4, 1997. www.physiol.ox.ac.uk/~jfs/pdf/stein&walsh.pdf.

17. Stein and Walsh, "To See but Not to Read."

18. Angela J. Fawcett, "Dyslexia and Literacy: Key Issues for Research," June 23, 2002. http://media.wiley.com/product_data/excerpt/45/04714863/0471486345.pdf.

19. Maryanne Wolf, "New Research on an Old Problem: A Brief History of Fluency," *Scholastic Reading Resources Network*. http://teacher.scholastic.com/reading/bestpractices/fluency/research.htm.

Chapter 3: Identifying Dyslexia

20. Shaywitz, *Overcoming Dyslexia*, p. 94.

21. Shaywitz, *Overcoming Dyslexia*, p. 94.

22. Thomas G. West, *In the Mind's Eye: Visual Thinkers, Gifted People with Dyslexia and Other Learning Difficulties, Computer Images, and the Ironies of Creativity.* Updated ed. Amherst, NY: Prometheus, 1997, p. 58.

23. Frank DeSena, interview by author, Redondo Beach, CA, April 5, 2004.

24. Snowling, *Dyslexia*, p. 89.

25. Shaywitz, *Overcoming Dyslexia*, p. 133.

26. Snowling, *Dyslexia*, p. 96.

27. Snowling, *Dyslexia*, p. 103.

28. Quoted in D'Arcangelo, "Learning About Learning to Read."

29. Dana, interview.

30. Shaywitz, *Overcoming Dyslexia*, p. 289.

31. Robert J. Sternberg and Elena L. Grigorenko, *Our Labeled Children: What Every Parent and Teacher Needs to Know About Learning Disabilities*. Reading, MA: Perseus, 1999, p. 7.

32. Priscilla Vail, "Priscilla Vail Speaks with SchwabLearning. org on Learning Styles & Emotions," SchwabLearning.org, 2003. www.schwablearning.org/pdfs/expert_vail.pdf?date= 9-22-03.

33. Shaywitz, *Overcoming Dyslexia*, p. 121.

34. West, *In the Mind's Eye*, pp. 56–57.

Chapter 4: Treating Dyslexia

35. National Reading Panel, *Teaching Children to Read: An Evidence-Based Assessment of the Scientific Research Literature on Reading and Its Implications for Reading Instruction*. NIH pub. no. 00-4769, National Institutes of Health, US Department of Health and Human Services, April 2000, p. 2–94.

36. Shaywitz, *Overcoming Dyslexia*, p. 293.

37. Joanne Lande, interview by author, Redondo Beach, CA, May 7, 2004.

38. DeSena, interview.

39. Susan Hall, "Susan Hall Speaks with SchwabLearning.org on Reading and Parental Involvement," SchwabLearning. org, 2002. www.schwablearning.org/pdfs/expert_hall.pdf? date=3-25-02.

40. Quoted in Shaywitz, *Overcoming Dyslexia*, p. 258.

41. Sheldon Horowitz, "The Discrepancy Formula: How the Aptitude Achievement Formula Keeps Educators from Doing Their Jobs," *Learning Disabilities Online.* www.ldonline.org/ld_indepth/assessment/horowitz_discrepancy_formula.html.

42. John Stein and Joel Talcott, "Impaired Neuronal Timing in Developmental Dyslexia—the Magnocellular Hypothesis," *Dyslexia*, 1999. www.physiol.ox.ac.uk/~jfs/pdf/dyslexiaj.pdf.

43. John J. Ratey, *A User's Guide to the Brain*. New York: Pantheon, 2001, p. 98.

Chapter 5: Living and Coping with Dyslexia

44. West, *In the Mind's Eye*, p. 56.
45. Quoted in Kurnoff, *The Human Side of Dyslexia*, pp. 237–38.
46. Robert Frank with Kathryn Livingston, *The Secret Life of the Dyslexic Child.* New York: Rodale, 2002, p. 155.
47. Quoted in Kurnoff, *The Human Side of Dyslexia*, p. 304.
48. Frank with Livingston, *The Secret Life of the Dyslexic Child*, p. 23.
49. Frank with Livingston, *The Secret Life of the Dyslexic Child*, p. 24.
50. Quoted in Kurnoff, *The Human Side of Dyslexia*, p. 242.
51. Quoted in Kurnoff, *The Human Side of Dyslexia*, p. 91.
52. Frank with Livingston, *The Secret Life of the Dyslexic Child*, p. 17.
53. Quoted in Joel Schwartz, "Dyslexic Kids' Brains Must Work Five Times Harder," *University of Washington*, October 4, 1999. www.washington.edu/newsroom/news/1999archive/10-99 archive/k100499a.html.
54. DeSena, interview.
55. Vail, "Priscilla Vail Speaks with SchwabLearning.org."
56. Quoted in Kurnoff, *The Human Side of Dyslexia*, p. 61.
57. Sondra, interview by author, Redondo Beach, CA, August 13, 2004. (Name changed to respect interviewee's privacy)
58. Quoted in Kurnoff, *The Human Side of Dyslexia*, p. 37.
59. Quoted in Kurnoff, *The Human Side of Dyslexia*, pp. 90–91.
60. Quoted in Kurnoff, *The Human Side of Dyslexia*, p. 88.
61. Melinda, interview by author, Torrance, CA, March 10, 2004. (Name changed to respect interviewee's privacy)
62. Quoted in Kurnoff, *The Human Side of Dyslexia*, p. 80.
63. Quoted in Kurnoff, *The Human Side of Dyslexia*, p. 304.
64. Frank with Livingston, *The Secret Life of the Dyslexic Child*, p. 154.
65. Quoted in Kurnoff, *The Human Side of Dyslexia*, p. 304.
66. Ellen Winner, "Uncommon Talents: Gifted Children, Prodigies, and Savants" in Editors of Scientific American Magazine, *The Scientific American Book of the Brain*. New York: Lyons, 1999, p. 84.

67. Winner, "Uncommon Talents," pp. 84-85.

68. Winner, "Uncommon Talents," p. 84.

69. West, *In the Mind's Eye,* p. 19.

70. West, *In the Mind's Eye,* p. 19.

71. Sternberg and Grigorenko, *Our Labeled Children*, p. 5.

72. Frank with Livingston, *The Secret Life of the Dyslexic Child,* p. 117.

Glossary

accommodations: Changes in the classroom or workplace made to help people with disabilities.

assessment: An evaluation of abilities and disabilities to determine the need for special education.

auditory: Related to hearing.

automatization: A term used to describe the process of making repeated tasks, such as typing, driving, or reading, automatic.

cerebellum: An area of the brain involved in the actions of muscles and body balance.

chromosome: A threadlike strand, containing genes, found in cells.

fine motor skills: Skills needed to coordinate the small muscles of the hand in tasks such as manipulating objects or writing.

functional magnetic resonance imaging (fMRI): A technique that uses radio waves to make images of an active brain.

gene: Genes are located on chromosomes in cells; each gene determines specific hereditary characteristics such as eye color or shape of a nose.

genome: The total genetic content in chromosomes.

gestation: The period of development from conception until birth.

individualized education program (IEP): A plan that specifies the educational services to be given to a student with a learning disability.

literacy: The ability to read and write.

magnocells: Large neurons that form the magnocellular pathways of vision located in the brain in the path from the eyes to the visual cortex area in the back of the brain.

multisensory: Involving multiple senses, such as vision, hearing, and touch.

neurological: Related to the brain or the spinal cord.

neurologist: A medical doctor who specializes in researching and treating disorders of the brain and nervous system.

opthalmologist: A medical doctor who specializes in treating diseases of the eye.

phoneme: The smallest unit of sound in a language.

phonemic awareness: The ability to recognize that words are made up of distinct sound units.

psychologist: A person trained to help people with behavioral or emotional issues. An educational or school psychologist is trained to assess learning disabilities and helps people with issues related to education.

remediation: The process of correcting a problem.

sequencing: Placing letters, words, numbers, and events in correct order.

social worker: A person trained to help people adjust to family and other social situations.

visual: Related to seeing.

Organizations to Contact

Dyslexia Awareness Resource Center (DARC)
928 Carpinteria St., Suite 2
Santa Barbara, CA 93103
(805) 963-7339
e-mail: info@dyslexiacenter.org
Web site: www.dyslexiacenter.org

DARC is a nonprofit institution that provides services to adults and children affected with dyslexia, attention disorders, and other learning disabilities. The center also conducts outreach and training seminars for literacy programs. The center maintains an extensive book, video, and audio library featuring materials on dyslexia, attention disorders, and other learning disabilities.

International Dyslexia Association (IDA)
(formerly the Orton Dyslexia Society)
8600 LaSalle Rd., Chester Bldg., Suite 382
Baltimore, MD 21286-3123
(410) 296-0232
e-mail: info@interdys.org
Web site: www.interdys.org

IDA is a nonprofit organization that provides support and information for people with dyslexia, their parents, educators, and researchers. IDA was founded in memory of neurologist Samuel T. Orton, who initiated dyslexia research in the United States. Information is available in English and Spanish on the Web site.

Learning Disabilities Association of America (LDA)
4156 Library Rd.

Pittsburgh, PA 15234
(412) 341-1515
(888) 300-6710
e-mail: info@ldaamerica.org
Web site: www.ldanatl.org

The LDA is a nonprofit volunteer organization that provides information and resources for people with learning disabilities. It encourages research and promotes public awareness of issues related to learning disabilities. The LDA is a leading advocate for laws and policies that create greater opportunities for people with learning disabilities.

National Association of Private Special Education Centers (NAPSEC)
1522 K St., NW, Suite 1032
Washington, DC 20005
(202) 408-3338
e-mail: napsec@aol.com
Web site: www.napsec.org

NAPSEC is a nonprofit association of private special education schools. The organization provides a free referral service to parents and professionals who are looking for an appropriate placement for children and clients with disabilities. NAPSEC also provides educational, scientific, and research materials regarding special education to parents of children with disabilities and the general public.

National Center for Learning Disabilities (NCLD)
381 Park Ave., South, Suite 1401
New York, NY 10016
(212) 545-7510
(888) 575-7373
Web site: www.ld.org

This nonprofit organization provides state-by-state referrals for services such as assessments, tutoring, and training for people with learning disabilities. The NCLD lobbies for the rights of people with learning disabilities and provides legislative updates.

Each year the NCLD provides a ten-thousand-dollar college scholarship for a high school student with a learning disability.

National Information Center for Children and Youth with Disabilities (NICHCY)
PO Box 1492
Washington, DC 20013-1492
(800) 695-0285
e-mail: nichcy@aed.org
Web site: www.nichcy.org

The NICHCY is an information and referral center that provides free information to the public on disabilities and disability-related issues.

Recording for the Blind and Dyslexic (RFB&D)
20 Roszel Rd.
Princeton, NJ 08540
(609) 452-0606
(800) 221-4792
e-mail: custserv@rfbd.org
Web site: www.rfbd.org

The RFB&D is a private organization that lends recorded textbooks and other educational materials to people who have trouble reading because of learning or physical disabilities. There is a registration fee and an annual membership fee for the RFB&D service.

For Further Reading

Books

Dale S. Brown, *Learning a Living: A Guide to Planning Your Career and Finding a Job for People with Learning Disabilities, Attention Deficit Disorder, and Dyslexia.* Bethesda, MD: Woodbine House, 2000. This book provides information and advice on pursuing careers for high school and college students as well as adults with dyslexia and other learning disabilities.

Rhoda Cummings and Gary Fisher, *The Survival Guide for Teenagers with LD.* Minneapolis: Free Spirit, 1993. This work provides tips for teenagers with learning disabilities on succeeding in school and making decisions for college, careers, and living as adults. It is also available on audio cassette.

Chris Hayhurst, *The Brain and Spinal Cord: Learning How We Think, Feel, and Move.* New York: Rosen, 2002. The author describes the brain and nervous system and includes detailed illustrations based on computer scans of human bodies.

Jonathan Mooney and David Cole, *Learning Outside the Lines.* New York: Fireside, 2000. Mooney, who is dyslexic, and Cole, who has ADHD, describe their experiences in school and how they overcame their disabilities and succeeded in college.

Penny Hutchins Paquette and Cheryl Gerson Tuttle, *Learning Disabilities: The Ultimate Teen Guide.* Lanham, MD: Scarecrow, 2003. The authors describe several learning disabilities, including dyslexia, and offer suggestions for overcoming the obstacles faced by teens with learning disabilities.

Gerard J. Sagmiller, *Dyslexia: My Life.* Smithville, MO: DML, 1995. The author describes how he dealt with his dyslexia and overcame the ignorance and prejudice of society to succeed in school and business.

Jennifer Viegas, *The Eye: Learning How We See.* New York: Rosen, 2002. This book describes the relationship of the eye to the brain and how people see. It contains detailed illustrations based on computer scans of human bodies.

Web Sites

Learning Disabilities Online (www.ldonline.org). This Web site contains articles written by educators, psychologists, and researchers on learning disabilities. It features Kidzone, an interactive area especially designed for children with learning disabilities. Kidzone contains fun activities and showcases children's art and writing. Information is also available in Spanish.

Schwab Learning (www.schwablearning.org). This site provides information on identifying and coping with learning difficulties. It features a message board where people can discuss their personal experiences with learning disabilities. It contains SparkTop.org, an interactive site for children eight to twelve years old.

Works Consulted

Books

Jackson Beatty, *The Human Brain: Essentials of Behavioral Neuroscience.* Thousand Oaks, CA: Sage, 2001. A comprehensive discussion of the brain and nervous system, including information on vision, language, learning, and associated disabilities.

Editors of *Scientific American* Magazine, *The Scientific American Book of the Brain.* New York: Lyons, 1999. This is a collection of articles exploring various aspects of the brain and consciousness. Includes chapters on language, learning, and giftedness.

Robert Frank with Kathryn Livingston, *The Secret Life of the Dyslexic Child.* New York: Rodale, 2002. This book, written by a dyslexic psychologist, describes what it feels like to have dyslexia and how parents can help their dyslexic children.

Daphne M. Hurford, *To Read or Not to Read.* New York: Simon & Schuster, Touchstone, 1999. Hurford, a reading and learning specialist, describes dyslexia and relates her personal experiences in helping dyslexics learn to read.

Shirley Kurnoff, *The Human Side of Dyslexia.* Monterey, CA: London Universal, 2001. Contains 142 interviews with dyslexic students, their parents, and siblings discussing the challenges and emotions related to dyslexia.

Mel Levine, *A Mind at a Time.* New York: Simon & Schuster, 2002. The author discusses the various ways in which all minds differ and recommends individualized methods for teaching.

National Reading Panel, *Teaching Children to Read: An Evidence-Based Assessment of the Scientific Research Literature on Reading and Its Implications for Reading Instruction.* NIHpub no. 00-4769,

National Institutes of Health, US Department of Health and Human Services, April 2000.

John J. Ratey, *A User's Guide to the Brain.* New York: Pantheon, 2001. This book discusses how the human brain processes perceptions, language, memory, and emotions.

Schwab Foundation for Learning, *Bridges to Learning: What to Do When You Suspect Your Child Has a Reading Problem.* San Mateo, CA: Schwab Foundation for Learning, 1999. This library edition is a bound book containing five booklets that describe what dyslexia is, how it is identified, and how dyslexics and their families can work with teachers and schools.

Sally E. Shaywitz, *Overcoming Dyslexia: A New and Complete Science-Based Program for Overcoming Reading Problems at Any Level.* New York: Knopf, 2003. A comprehensive look at what dyslexia is, its cause and diagnosis, and the best methods for its remediation.

Lawrence M. Siegel, *The Complete IEP Guide: How to Advocate for Your Special Ed Child.* Berkeley, CA: Nolo, 2001. This guide explains legal aspects of individualized educational programs.

Margaret J. Snowling, *Dyslexia.* 2nd ed. Oxford, UK: Blackwell, 2000. This book reviews and discusses research on dyslexia, including its neurological causes and methods of assessment.

Robert J. Sternberg and Elena L. Grigorenko, *Our Labeled Children: What Every Parent and Teacher Needs to Know About Learning Disabilities.* Reading, MA: Perseus, 1999. The authors argue that everyone has both abilities and disabilities and recommend methods of diagnosing and remediating learning disabilities in keeping with their view.

Thomas G. West, *In the Mind's Eye: Visual Thinkers, Gifted People with Dyslexia and Other Learning Difficulties, Computer Images, and the Ironies of Creativity.* Updated ed. Amherst, NY: Prometheus, 1997. This work explores the idea of seeing dyslexics as people with visual and spatial abilities as opposed to only seeing them as having language disabilities.

Periodicals

B. Bower, "Dyslexia's DNA Clue," *Science News*, August 30, 2003.

Christine Gorman, "The New Science of Dyslexia," *Time*, July 28, 2003.

Laura Helmuth, "Dyslexia: Same Brains, Different Language," *Science*, March 16, 2001.

E. Paulesu et al., "Dyslexia: Cultural Diversity and Biological Unity," *Science*, March 16, 2001.

Internet Sources

Beth Azar, "What's the Link Between Speed and Reading in Children with Dyslexia?" *Monitor on Psychology*, March 2000. www. apa.org/monitor/mar00/dyslexia.html.

British Dyslexia Association, "Unrecognised Dyslexia and the Route to Offending," June 16, 2004. www.bda-dyslexia.org. uk/ main/campaigning/doc/dyslexia_and_youth_offending. pdf.

Colorado Learning Disabilities Research Center, "Project I: Twin Studies." http://psych.colorado.edu/~willcutt/CLDRC/project 1.htm.

Marcia D'Arcangelo, "Learning About Learning to Read: A Conversation with Sally Shaywitz," *Educational Leadership*, October 1999. www.ascd.org/publications/ed_lead/199910/darcangelo.html.

Drake D. Duane, "Defining Dyslexia," *Mayo Clinic Proceedings*, November 2001. www.mayo.edu/proceedings/2001/nov/76 11e1.pdf.

Angela J. Fawcett, "Dyslexia and Literacy: Key Issues for Research," June 23, 2002. http://media.wiley.com/product_ data/excerpt/45/04714863/0471486345.pdf.

Susan Hall, "Susan Hall Speaks with SchwabLearning.org on Reading and Parental Involvement," *SchwabLearning.org*, 2002. www.schwablearning.org/pdfs/expert_hall.pdf?date=3-25-02.

Sheldon Horowitz, "The Discrepancy Formula: How the Aptitude-Achievement Formula Keeps Educators from Doing Their Jobs," *Learning Disabilities Online*. www.ldonline.org/ld_in depth/ assessment/horowitz_discrepancy_formula.html.

Slava Katusic et al., "Incidence of Reading Disability in a Population-Based Birth Cohort, 1976–1982, Rochester, Minn.," *Mayo Clinic*

Proceedings. November 2001. www.mayo.edu/proceedings/2001/nov/7611a1.pdf.

Raymond Klein, "Observations on the Temporal Correlates of Reading Failure," *Reading and Writing: An Interdisciplinary Journal,* 2002. www.linguistics.pomona.edu/thornton/lgcs 185c/readings/Klein02.pdf.

G. Reid Lyon, "Why Johnny Can't Decode," *Washington Post,* October 27, 1996. www.ldonline.org/ld_indepth/reading/why_johnny_cant_decode.html.

———, "Why Reading Is Not a Natural Process," *Learning Disabilities Association of America,* January/February 2000. www. ld online.org/(ld_indepth/reading/why_reading_is_not.html.

National Information Center for Children and Youth with Disabilities, "Individualized Education Program," September 1999. www.nichcy.org/pubs/ideapubs/lg2.pdf.

———, "Reading and Learning Disabilities," February 2004. www.nichcy.org/pubs/factshe/fs17.pdf.

Radiological Society of North America, "Functional MR Imaging (fMRI)—Brain," *Radiology Info.,* September 10, 2003. www. radiologyresource.org/content/functional_mr.htm.

Franck Ramus, "The Neural Basis of Reading Acquisition," in *The New Cognitive Neurosciences.* Ed. M.S. Gazzaniga. 3rd ed. Cambridge, MA: MIT Press. www.ehess.fr/centres/lscp/persons/ramus/TCNS3.pdf.

Franck Ramus et al., "Theories of Developmental Dyslexia: Insights from a Multiple Case Study of Dyslexic Adults." 2002. http://cogprints.ecs.soton.ac.uk/archive/00002350/01/dyslexia02web.pdf.

John Schacter, "Reading Programs That Work: A Review of Programs for Pre-Kindergarten to 4th Grade," October 25, 1999. www.mff.org/pubs/ME279.pdf.

Joel Schwartz, "Dyslexic Kids' Brains Must Work Five Times Harder," *University of Washington,* October 4, 1999. www.washington.edu/newsroom/news/1999/archive/10-99archive/K100499a.html.

Emily Staats, "Making the Transition," *LD Online*, January 1, 2001. www.ldonline.org/article.php?max=20&special_group ing=0&id=0&loc=11&start=41&end=60&sortby=lastupdate& show_abstract=1.

John Stein and Joel Talcott, "Impaired Neuronal Timing in Developmental Dyslexia—the Magnocellular Hypothesis," *Dyslexia*, 1999. www.physiol.ox.ac.uk/~jfs/pdf/dyslexiaj.pdf.

John Stein, Joel Talcott, and Vincent Walsh, "Controversy About the Visual Magnocellular Deficit in Developmental Dyslexics," *Trends in Cognitive Science*, June 2000. www.physiol.ox.ac. uk/~jfs/pdf/tics.pdf.

John Stein and Vincent Welsh, "To See but Not to Read: The Magnocellular Theory of Dyslexia," *Trends in Neuroscience*, November 4, 1997. www.physiol.ox.ac.uk/~jfs/pdf/stein&walsh.pdf.

Lindsey Tanner, "Dyslexia Found More Common in Boys than Girls," *San Diego Union-Tribune*. April 28, 2004. www.signon sandiego.com/uniontrib/20040428/news_ln28dyslexia.html.

Elise Temple et al., "Neural Deficits in Children with Dyslexia Ameliorated by Behavioral Remediation: Evidence from Functional MRI," *Proceedings of the National Academy of Sciences*, March 4, 2003. www.pnas.org/cgi/reprint/100/5/2860.pdf.

Priscilla Vail, "Priscilla Vail Speaks with SchwabLearning.org on Learning Styles & Emotions," *SchwabLearning.org*, 2003. www. schwablearning.org/pdfs/expert_vail.pdf?date=9-22-03.

Maryanne Wolf, "New Research on an Old Problem: A Brief History of Fluency," *Scholastic Reading Resources Network.* http:// teacher.scholastic.com/reading/bestpractices/fluency/re search.htm.

Web Sites

Dragon NaturallySpeaking (www.dragontalk.com). This site gives information about Dragon NaturallySpeaking, a voice-recognition software.

Kurzweil Educational Systems (www.kurzweiledu.com). Kurzweil is the maker of the Kurzweil system, a text-to-speech reading aid.

Lindamood-Bell Learning Processes (www.lblp.com). This site gives information about LiPS, the multisensory reading program.

National Center for Educational Statistics (http://nces.ed.gov). The U.S. Department of Education maintains statistics regarding education, including reading performance of students in public and private schools, on this site.

Scientific Learning Corporation (www.scilearn.com). Scientific Learning is the maker of Fast ForWord, a reading remediation program.

Wizcom Technologies (www.wizcomtec.com). Wizcom is the maker of the portable Reading Pen.

Index

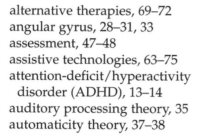

alternative therapies, 69–72
angular gyrus, 28–31, 33
assessment, 47–48
assistive technologies, 63–75
attention-deficit/hyperactivity
  disorder (ADHD), 13–14
auditory processing theory, 35
automaticity theory, 37–38

Berlin, Rudolph, 23–25
Bowers, Patricia, 39–40
brain
  impairments, 23, 39
  studies, 27–32, 69, 76
Broca's area, 29–31

causes, 40
cerebellar theory, 37–38
computer-based programs,
  61–62

DeSena, Frank, 66, 77
diagnosis
  of adults, 53–54
  assessment, 47–48
  discrepancy model, 68
  early, importance of, 55, 67
  effects of, 56
  IQ tests and, 14–15
  role of schools in, 45–46
  testing, 47–53
directional concepts, 12

discrepancy model, 14, 68
double deficit theory, 39
drug therapies, 72
dyslexia, 7, 10, 22
  as a gift, 87–88
  incidence of, 19–20
  as learning disability, 20–21
  origin of word, 10, 23–24, 25
dyslexics
  adult
    reading and, 44–45
    remediation and, 62–63
    workplace accommodations
      for, 84–85
  families of, 78–83
  famous, 8, 87–88
  reading difficulty of, 10–15,
    19–21
  talents of, 85–86
dyspraxia, 12
DYXC1 gene, 18

education laws, 59
emotional effects, 73–78, 82

Fast ForWord, 61–62, 69
fatigue, 76
Fawcett, Angela J., 37–38
Frank, Robert, 74–75, 88
frustration, 73–74
functional MRI (fMRI), 28–34,
  36, 53, 69

genetics, 15–18, 72
Gillingham, Anna, 25, 60
Grigorenko, Elena L., 55, 88

Hall, Susan, 67
heredity, 15–18
Hinshelwood, James, 24–25
Horowitz, Sheldon H., 68

individualized education
  program (IEP), 8, 57–59
Individuals with Disabilties
  Education Act, 68
IQ tests, 14–15
Irlen method, 70–71

Kurzweil system, 65
Kussmaul, Adolf, 23, 25

labeling, problems with, 54–55
Lande, Joanne, 63–64
language processing centers,
  28–33
learning disabilities, 20–21
Lindamood Phonemic
  Sequencing (LiPS) Program, 60
Lyon, G. Reid, 21

magnocellular pathways, 31–32,
  36
magnocellular theory, 39
math, difficult for dyslexics, 13
Moats, Louisa, 68
Morgan, W. Pringle, 24–25
motor skills, 12, 37–38, 69
movement therapies, 69
MRI technology, 27–28
  see also functional MRI
multisensory programs, 60

National Institute of Child
  Health and Human
  Development (NICHD), 21–22

National Reading Panel (NRP),
  59
nutritional therapies, 72

Orton, Samuel, 25–26, 60
Orton-Gillingham method, 60

phonemic awareness, 59–60
phonemic awareness tests,
  48–49
phonemic deficit theory, 33–35
phonics, 59–60

Ramus, Franck, 35
reading, learning and, 42, 45–46,
  59–60
reading comprehension tests, 50
Reading Pen, 65
reading tests, 49–50
remediation
  for adults, 62–63
  challenges in, 68
  computer-based programs,
    61–62
  multisensory programs, 60
  results of, 69
  role of schools in, 57–59
  success, factors in, 66–68
research, 22
  brain imaging, 27–32
  early, 23–25
  language, role of, 26–27

school, difficulty in, 20–21,
  42–44, 75–77, 83–84
self-esteem, 75
sequencing, 13
Shaywitz, Sally
  on brain studies, 29–31
  on diagnosis, 50, 53–55
  on dyslexic children, 7, 9
  on fMRI technology, 34
  on remediation, 63

on symptoms, 41–42
Snowling, Margaret, 34, 49, 50
spelling, 11, 42
spelling tests, 50–51
Stein, John, 36, 39, 69–70
Sternberg, Robert J., 55, 88
symptoms, 10–14, 41–45

Talcot, Joel, 69–70
tests. *See specific tests*
text-to-speech programs, 65
theories, 39–40
  see also specific theories
treatment
  accommodations, 83–85
  assistive technologies and,
    63–66
  emotional support in, 83
  future of, 72
  success, factors in, 66–68, 82,

85–87
  see also remediation; *and specific*
    therapies
twins study, 15–17

Vail, Priscilla, 55, 77
visual processing theory, 36
visual therapies, 69–71
voice-recognition software, 65

Walsh, Vincent, 36, 39
Wernicke's area, 29–31, 33–34
West, Thomas, 45, 56, 74, 87
Winner, Ellen, 86–87
Wolf, Maryanne, 39–40
word processing, 63–64
workplace accommodations,
  84–85

Picture Credits

About the Author

Arda Darakjian Clark holds a master's degree in English. She has worked for many years as a technical writer, writing procedure and system-user manuals. She has also worked on various projects as a freelance writer and editor. She lives in Redondo Beach, California, with her husband and children.